Judy Vidican

Terminology
for Accountants

A project sponsored by

THE COMMITTEE ON ACCOUNTING

AND AUDITING RESEARCH

of

THE CANADIAN INSTITUTE

OF CHARTERED ACCOUNTANTS

1 9 6 2

The Canadian Institute of Chartered Accountants
250 Bloor Street East   —   Toronto 5

generally accepted accounting principles applied on a basis consistent with that of the preceding year. 2. Any written report by an auditor in accordance with the terms of his appointment.

Authorized capital. The number and par value of shares of each class having a par value and the number of shares of each class without nominal or par value that a company may issue as determined by its act of incorporation, letters patent, memorandum of association, or otherwise.

Average cost. Cost of stores issued, cost of goods sold, or inventory cost, determined by applying a weighted average of the prices at which goods were included in the opening inventory and the prices of acquisitions during the period. The average cost may be recomputed at the time of each acquisition or computed periodically at other appropriate times, e.g. at the year end.

B

Back order. The part of an original order for goods or services from a customer that remains to be filled after a portion of the original order has been completed.

Bad debt. An account or note receivable that is uncollectible. (Compare **Doubtful account** or **Debt**.)

Bad debts recovered. Collections on accounts previously written off as bad debts.

Balance. *n.* The excess of debits over credits or credits over debits, as the case may be.

Balance. *v.* 1. To determine that the totals of the debit and credit balances in books of account kept by double entry are equal. 2. To determine that the total of the balances of the accounts in a subsidiary ledger is in agreement with the balance of the controlling account.

Balance sheet. A formal statement of financial position, in the form of a concise statement compiled from books of account, showing assets, liabilities, and owners' equity in classified manner and as at a particular moment of time. The balance sheet is a statement of current resources, unexpired costs, liabilities to be met and sources of ownership funds, rather than a statement of worth.

Balance sheet audit. An examination sufficient to provide the basis for an expression of opinion as to whether the balance sheet presents a fair view of the financial position of the enterprise, usually without implying any extensive examination of the records of transactions for the period; an examination of position rather than transactions.

Balance sheet, Form of. The arrangement of the items in the balance sheet, for example: (a) *Account form*—The assets are set on one side with the liabilities and owners' equity on the other. The total of the assets appears as an amount equal to the total of the liabilities and owners' equity. (b) *Double account form*—The balance sheet is shown in two sections, (1) the Capital Account containing those accounts relative to the cost of fixed assets, long-term liabilities, permanently invested capital, and the balancing amount which is carried to the General Account, and (2) the General Account containing current assets and liabilities, earned surplus, and the balancing amount carried from the Capital Account and any remaining items. The method is now rarely used except in Britain, although a similar procedure is generally followed in fund accounting by municipalities and some other public bodies. (c) *Report form*—The liabilities are deducted from the assets to show the owners' equity as the balance.

Balance sheet equation. The formula expressing the fundamental balance sheet relationships, namely, Assets = Liabilities + Owners' equity (or a variation of this formula, e.g. $A - L = O$). The balance sheet equation is used to explain the equality of debits and credits in double entry bookkeeping.

Bank confirmation. A statement obtained by an auditor from his client's banker reporting the position, at a stated date, of the client's bank accounts, loans and other liabilities, security held against liabilities, and other matters.

Bank discount. The amount deducted by a bank from the face amount or maturity value of a note, representing interest paid in advance.

Bank statement. A list sent by a bank periodically (usually monthly) to its customers setting out all of the changes during the period in the customer's current or personal chequing account with the bank. The cheques charged against the account during the period are usually returned to the customer with the bank statement together with vouchers for other entries, if any, initiated by the bank.

Bankrupt. *adj.* The legal status of an individual or company who has made an assignment or against whom a receiving order has been made.

Bankruptcy. *n.* The state of being bankrupt. (Compare **Insolvency.**)

Base stock method. An inventory valuation procedure, under which a predetermined minimum stock of materials or merchandise is carried in the inventory continuously at a fixed price.

Bear. *n.* An investor who believes that security or commodity prices are due to decline and sells securities or commodities with this in mind. (Compare **Bull.**)

Bearer security. A security not registered in the name of any person or on which the only or last endorsement is in blank (the latter security is commonly said to be in "street" form). Physical possession of the security can establish ownership.

Beneficial owner. The real owner of an asset, usually a security, title to which is registered in the name of a trustee.

Betterment. See Improvement.

Bill. *v.* To render an account, i.e. to send an invoice or periodic statement.

Bill of exchange. An unconditional order in writing, addressed by one person to another, signed by the person giving it, requiring the person to whom it is addressed to pay, on demand or at a fixed or determinable future time, a sum certain in money to or to the order of a specified person, or to bearer.

Bill of lading. A memorandum given by carriers acknowledging the receipt of goods and which serves as a document of title to the goods consigned.

Bill payable. A draft or promissory note payable. Generally used in the plural (bills payable) to distinguish drafts and notes from open accounts payable.

Bill receivable. A draft or promissory note receivable. Generally used in the plural (bills receivable) to distinguish drafts and notes from open accounts receivable.

Binary system. A number system using the base two, as opposed to the decimal number system which uses the base ten. The binary system is often used in mechanical and electronic data processing systems.

Blanket coverage. Protection under a contract of insurance afforded a class of property or persons which may fluctuate in quantity, quality or location.

Blocked currency. Currency which by law cannot be withdrawn from the issuing country or exchanged for the currency of another country.

Blotter. A simple record, e.g. a day book, sometimes made as the transactions occur, to provide the information required for subsequent formal entries.

Board of directors. 1. Persons elected by the shareholders of a limited company and responsible for supervising the affairs of the company.

11

2. Generally, persons elected by the members of an organization to be responsible for supervising its affairs.

Bond. 1. A certificate of indebtedness, issued by a government or company, generally being one of several or many such certificates. The term usually implies that assets have been pledged as security. (Compare **Debenture.**) 2. An obligation in writing, sometimes supported by collateral, given by an individual or company to another individual or company to pay damages, or to indemnify against losses caused by a third person through non-performance of a contract or other duties or by defalcation, e.g. a fidelity bond on a cashier or other employee of a business.

Bonus. A special payment or benefit made in addition to whatever is ordinarily arranged or contracted for, e.g. an extra payment to an employee, securities issued as a premium on the issue and sale of bonds or shares, special dividends in excess of customary rates.

Book debt. See **Account receivable.**

Book inventory. The stock of merchandise, raw materials, and supplies presumably on hand, as shown by the bookkeeping records.

Book of account. Any book or record in which business transactions of an enterprise or organization are recorded in terms of money and which constitutes part of the accounting system. The books of account include books of original entry as well as ledgers.

Book of original entry. A book of account in which business transactions are recorded preparatory to posting to ledger accounts.

Book profit. 1. Profit as shown by accounting records kept on the basis of sound accounting principles; contrasted with economic profit or profit computed on some other basis. 2. (*colloq.*) Unrealized profit.

Book value. 1. The amount at which an item appears in the books of account and financial statements. It should not be confused with the basis on which the amount is determined, e.g. cost, replacement cost, liquidation value. The term is not an appropriate description of a basis of valuation of assets. 2. In connection with owners' equity in a business, the amount of the net assets of the business shown in a balance sheet prepared in accordance with sound accounting principles.

Bookkeeping. The process of classifying and recording business transactions in terms of money in the books of account. (Compare **Accounting.**)

Bordereau. 1. An abstract or digest. 2. (*insurance*) A summary of insurance written.

Break-even point. The level of operations of a business at which revenues

12

PREFACE

The ready acceptance and strong demand for **Accounting Terminology** by accountants and non-accountants alike, have left little doubt as to the need for such a book. Since its publication in 1957, three printings have been exhausted and the only comments that have been made in regard to its contents were requests for the expansion of the areas covered to take in the lexicon of accountants rather than limiting the words defined to those relating directly to accounting.

Terminology for Accountants is a revised and expanded successor to **Accounting Terminology.** This book attempts to meet the requests noted above, at least partially, and this wider coverage is implied in the new title as well as in the fact that 854 words are defined in this edition, as opposed to 517 in the previous book.

In preparing this book, four objectives were kept in mind:

1. All of the definitions and references contained in **Accounting Terminology** have been reviewed to ensure that any changes of usage have been properly reflected. In doing this, we have tried to make some definitions more precise while, at the same time, eliminating quotations from other sources.

2. Words, not necessarily relating to accounting but in general use by accountants, have been added. Many words are included that might be considered to be primarily legal or economic in their connotations; however, with the greatly expanding roles that members of our profession are playing in business, these words are properly included in the very wide range of words used by accountants. Only words that have a specialized meaning to accountants have been included and then, generally, only those specialized meanings are defined. For example, **Commitment** has only its two business definitions set out in this book although it also has the (what I believe to be non-business) meaning of "imprisonment".

   In addition, no attempt has been made to encompass all, or even part of, legal phraseology. Legal definitions and references to statutes are included only if they form part of the normal vocabulary of accountants.

3. Most words with technical or semi-technical meanings are included but, for the most part, we have tried to cross-reference synonyms to one definition, and thus avoid repeating definitions.

4. The definitions given are an attempt at a **concise** description of the words or phrases covered. This book is designed as a dictionary rather than an encyclopedia.

This present edition has been based firmly on **Accounting Terminology** whose preparation was the responsibility of many leaders of our profession but, particularly, reflects the work and experience of my predecessor, Lawrence Macpherson, F.C.A. Of the many studies he initiated and carried through as Director of Research, few can have had so much beneficial effect for so many people in so many spheres as has **Accounting Terminology.**

Terminology for Accountants has been prepared largely by the Institute's research staff and most of the credit (in its non-accounting sense) for the final result is due to Gertrude Mulcahy, F.C.A. and Lorne Reesor, C.A. All members of the 1960-61 and 1961-62 Committees on Accounting and Auditing Research have reviewed drafts and, as in all projects on which they have worked, their co-operation and care have been in the best tradition of the high standards of past members of the Committee.

I would especially like to thank P. H. Lyons, C.A., I. E. Millie, C.A., A. W. Quayle, F.C.A., H. D. Rendall, C.A., J. S. Swinden, F.C.A., for their diligence and thought in reviewing particular parts of the manuscripts.

R. D. Thomas, F.C.A.,
Director of Research.

Toronto
May, 1962

ABBREVIATIONS USED

abbr.	abbreviation
adj.	adjective
Br.	British usage
colloq.	colloquial
math.	mathematical
n.	noun
obs.	obsolete
pl.	plural
U.S.	United States' usage
v.	verb
v.i.	intransitive verb
v.t.	transitive verb

A

Abatement. 1. The reduction of an expenditure. 2. The deduction of minor revenues incidental to an operation in calculating the cost of the operation.

Access time. (*machine accounting*) The time interval between the call for information from a storage unit and its delivery.

Accommodation party. A person who has signed a bill of exchange as drawer, acceptor or endorser, without receiving value therefor, for the purpose of lending his name to some other person.

Account. *n.* 1. A formal record of an asset, liability, proprietorship, revenue, or expense, in which the effects of transactions are indicated in terms of money or some other unit of measurement. 2. A statement setting out a summary of the transactions in terms of money between individuals and/or organizations for a stated period. 3. (*obs.*) A financial statement. 4. (*pl.*) Bookkeeping records in general. 5. (*pl.*) Collective term for the whole set of financial statements of a business enterprise, e.g. the annual accounts.

Account. *v.* 1. To render a statement of account. 2. To answer or explain (with *for*).

Account current. An account of mutual dealings and transactions between two persons, rendered by one to the other. Use of the term is generally limited to a statement of account between principal and agent, e.g. the statement of account rendered by a consignee to the consignor. (Compare **Current account.**)

Account form (of statement). An arrangement of statement items in the form of an account, in two balanced columns. See **Balance sheet, Form of.** (Compare **Report form.**)

Account payable. An amount owing to a creditor. Generally limited to a liability for purchases of goods or services. In statement presentation, accounts payable may include open accounts and notes. See also **Trade account payable.**

Account receivable. An amount claimed against a debtor, usually money rights arising from the sale of goods or services. In statement presentation, accounts receivable may include open accounts and notes. See also **Trade account receivable.**

Account sales. A statement rendered to a consignor of merchandise by the consignee giving particulars such as the sales of the consigned merchandise, amount of any such merchandise remaining unsold, gross

1

proceeds, expenses incurred by the consignee, consignee's commission, and net amount due to the consignor.

Accountability. The liability or obligation to render an accounting.

Accountancy. 1. Accounting theory and practice as a whole. 2. The accounting profession. 3. (*colloq.*) See **Accounting** 1.

Accountant. A person skilled in accounting.

Accounting. *n.* 1. The process of analysing and systematically recording, in terms of money, business transactions and events which are, in part at least, of a financial nature, and of summarizing, reporting and interpreting the results thereof. (Compare **Bookkeeping.**) 2. A formal report of the manner in which a responsibility has been discharged, e.g. an accounting by an agent to his principal or by an executor to the court.

Accounting control. See **Control** 2.

Accounting manual. A detailed description of the accounting policies of an organization, usually including an outline of the official procedures, forms, and responsibilities.

Accounting period. That period of time for which financial statements are prepared, e.g. week, month, year.

Accounting principle. 1. A concept recognized as a guiding factor of sound accounting. 2. (*pl.*) A body of concepts which have evolved over the years as the basis of sound accounting, (usually together with rules, conventions and practices recognized as appropriate methods of applying such basic concepts in particular circumstances). The term is not used in the sense of a set of hard and fast rules but rather of rules of general application which provide guides in the selection of accounting methods appropriate in particular circumstances.

Accounting procedures. The techniques and methods used in accounting; the specific practices followed in applying the basic concepts of sound accounting.

Accounting system. The methods of accounting used in an organization, including the procedures for recording, verifying, and reporting transactions.

Accounting unit. An enterprise, or a department, section, or branch for which a separate set of accounts is maintained.

Accrual basis of accounting. That method of recording transactions by which revenues and expenses are reflected in the accounts in the period in which they are considered to have been earned and incurred, respectively, whether or not such transactions have been finally settled by the receipt or payment of cash or its equivalent. (Compare **Cash basis of accounting.**)

Accrue. *v.i.* 1. To increase, to be added as increase. 2. (*legal*) To come into existence as an enforceable claim or to vest as a right.

Accrue. *v.t.* In accounting usage, to record that which has increased with the passage of time or the rendering or receiving of service, e.g. interest, taxes, royalties, wages.

Accrued asset. A developing but not yet enforceable claim against another person which is accumulating with the passage of time or the rendering of service. It arises from the sale of services (including the use of money) which have been only partly performed at the time of accounting and hence are not billable.

Accrued expense. An expense which has been incurred in an accounting period but for which no enforceable claim will be made in that accounting period by the person who rendered the service. It arises from the purchase of services (including the use of money) which have been only partly performed at the time of accounting and hence are not yet billed or paid for.

Accrued liability. A developing but not yet enforceable claim by another person, which is accumulating with the passage of time or the receipt of service. It arises from the purchase of services (including the use of money) which have been only partly performed at the time of accounting and hence are not yet billed or paid for.

Accrued revenue. Revenue which has been earned in an accounting period but for which no enforceable claim will be made in that accounting period against the person for whom the service was rendered. It arises from the sale of services (including the use of money) which have been only partly performed at the time of accounting and hence are not yet billable.

Accumulated depreciation. The total credit resulting from charges for depreciation on fixed assets since the assets were placed in use by a business. This total is normally deducted from the cost of the related fixed assets on the balance sheet.

Accumulated earnings. See **Earned surplus.**

Acid test ratio. The ratio of the total of such of an organization's cash, accounts receivable and marketable securities as are properly included in its current assets to its total current liabilities. This ratio provides an indication of the organization's ability to meet its current obligations

Actual cost

quickly without resorting to any realization of its assets other than in the normal course of its operations. (Compare **Current ratio.**)

Actual cost. See Historic cost.

Adjusting entry. 1. An entry made before closing the books for the period, to apportion amounts of revenue or expense to accounting periods or to operating divisions, e.g. apportionment of administrative expenses between departments, or wages between accounting periods when the current period ends between two paydays, or rental revenue when the rental revenue account includes an amount applying to tenancy in a subsequent period. 2. A correcting entry.

Administration expenses.
Administrative expenses. The classification for financial statement purposes of those expenses of an organization relating to the overall direction of its affairs; as opposed to those expenses incurred for other specialized functions, such as manufacturing, selling or financing.

Administrator. 1. A person who manages the affairs of an organization. 2. A technical (legal) term given to a court-appointed person who manages the estate of a deceased person. (Compare **Executor.**)

Ad valorem. A method of levying a tax or duty on goods by using their estimated value as the tax base.

Advance. *n.* 1. A payment that is to be accounted for by the recipient at some later date, e.g. payment for expenses to be incurred. 2. A payment made on account of, but before completion of, a contract, or before receipt of goods or services. 3. A loan.

Affiliated company. 1. A company related to another by ownership, management or some other method of control. 2. A company related to another company in a manner defined by legislation for particular purposes.

Agent. An individual or company employed by another individual or company (the principal) for the purpose of making contracts between the principal and third individuals or companies. (Compare **Broker.**)

Aging. A process of analysis of receivables by classifying the amounts according to the length of time for which they have been outstanding or for which they have been due. The time may be measured from the billing date or from the due date for each amount.

Allied company. See Associated company.

All-inclusive income statement. A method of statement presentation where all transactions affecting operations, whether current or not, are shown in the statement of profit and loss. Only the net profit or loss for the current

4

period, dividends declared and appropriations authorized in the period are set out in the earned surplus statement. (Compare **Current operating concept.**)

Allocate. 1. To apportion or spread a debit or credit to appropriate accounts, e.g. to charge a rental payment to various departments depending on the floor space of the rented premises occupied by each. 2. (*government accounting*) To authorize a budgeted appropriation for a particular function.

Allocation. The process or result of allocating.

Allotment. 1. In corporate accounting the acceptance of subscriptions for shares or bonds. 2. (*government accounting*) A sub-division of a budget appropriation, according to activity, object of expenditure, or time period.

Allowance. 1. A rebate or reduction in respect of a sale of goods or services, e.g. an allowance to compensate for damage to goods in transit or failure of goods to meet a specified quality. 2. A deduction from the stated value of assets to reduce them to the estimated realizable value or to indicate that portion of the value thereof that has been charged to costs and expenses. 3. An amount paid to an employee or agent under an arrangement in respect of expenses.

Alteration. A change in or a modification of a fixed asset.

Alternative cost. See **Opportunity cost.**

Amalgamation. The fusion of two or more companies by transfer of their assets and liabilities to a new company or by transfer of the assets and liabilities to one of the existing companies. The latter process is more particularly called a **merger.**

Amortization. 1. The gradual writing off of a balance in an account, such as an expenditure on a patent right or alterations to leased premises, over an appropriate period. A common example is the writing off of a premium on bonds over the term of the bonds. Depreciation accounting is a form of amortization applied to tangible fixed assets. Depletion accounting is another form of amortization, applied to natural resources such as mineral deposits or timber limits which are subject to exhaustion. 2. The gradual extinction or provision for extinction of a debt by serial redemption or sinking fund payments.

Analyze. To examine the composition of an item (such as a balance in an account) usually by summarizing its constituent elements, generally with explanations and references to supporting evidence.

Annual report. The information provided annually by the directors of a limited company, or the management of an organization, to the shareholders, owners, or other interested parties concerning operations and financial position. Usually, it comprises the annual financial statements, the auditor's report thereon, and the reports of officers or directors.

Annual return.

Annual summary. The information required to be filed annually with the Department of the Secretary of State under *The Companies Act* (Canada) as to shares, debentures, shareholders' meetings, directors, etc., or a similar return required under the statutes of a province.

Apportionment. 1. The division and allocation or distribution of an amount in proportionate parts. 2. (*executorship accounting*) The allocation of receipts and disbursements to income and corpus (capital), in order to determine the respective interests of life tenants and remaindermen.

Appraisal. A valuation, especially of land, buildings, machinery, and equipment, made by individuals or firms qualified as expert in such valuations. The valuation may be made on one of several bases, e.g. replacement cost, replacement cost less observed depreciation, market value.

Appraisal surplus. (*obs.*) The credit result of increasing the recorded value of fixed assets as the result of an appraisal. It is now more generally accepted to use a description such as "Excess of appraised value of fixed assets over cost". See **Appraisal.**

Appreciation. Increase in value over cost or book value. Generally, the term refers to increases resulting from external influences such as rising prices rather than to increases resulting from utility added by action of the owner.

Appropriated earned surplus. See **Earned surplus.**

Appropriation. 1. A setting aside of net profit or of accumulated earnings to an account, e.g. a transfer of earned surplus to a general contingency reserve or to a sinking fund reserve. 2. An authorization to make expenditures, usually limited in amount and time. 3. (*government accounting*) An approved budget estimate, which may limit expenditures but which does not by itself constitute authorization to make expenditures.

Appropriation account. 1. (*Br.*) An account to which net profits are carried and from which transfers are made to reflect the disposition of such profits. 2. Used to some extent in partnership and sole proprietorship accounts in the sense similar to the British usage. The equivalent term in limited company accounts is generally "earned surplus" account. 3. An account for a budget estimate, especially in government accounting. See **Appropriation ledger.**

6

Appropriation ledger. In budgetary accounting, especially for governments, a subsidiary ledger containing an account for each appropriation. Usually each account shows the original appropriation, subsequent transfers, encumbrances and expenditures, and unencumbered and unexpended balances.

Arm's length. *adj.* 1. (*income tax*) A type of relationship between persons involved in a business transaction. The precise meaning of the relationship is dependent upon the taxing statute and interpretation thereof. 2. (*colloq.*) A general term applied to any transaction where the parties to the transaction are independent of each other.

Arrangement. 1. The action of planning or settling details. 2. The result of a proposal under *The Companies' Creditors Arrangement Act* (Canada). 3. (*statistics*) Any ordering of "n" objects.

Articles of association. The internal regulations of a limited company incorporated by registration; analogous to the by-laws of a limited company incorporated by letters patent. See **By-law** 2.

Assessment. 1. A notice of an amount due from a special group, e.g. a club or similar organization may make an assessment on its members to raise money in addition to the amount raised by its regular fees. 2. (*government accounting*) The process of determining the amount of a (tax) levy, or the notice of the amount of a (tax) levy. In the case of a municipal real property tax, the assessment is the value for taxation purposes placed on the property to be taxed (and an "assessment notice" informs the taxpayer of this valuation) while the notice of the amount of tax to be paid is usually called the "tax notice" or "tax bill". 3. (*colloq.*) (*income tax*) The notice of assessment sent to the taxpayer informing him of the amount of tax levied.

Asset. 1. In general, a thing of value owned. In accounting, something that is measurable in terms of money and represented by a debit balance that may properly be included in a balance sheet in accordance with accepted accounting principles. 2. A sole right, acquired in the past, to an expected future benefit or benefits.

Associated company. A company operating either wholly or partially in co-operation with another by reason of common control, contract, or agreement. The term includes affiliated companies. A more specialized meaning may be given to the term by statutory definition for taxation or corporate purposes.

Associated corporation. (*income tax*) A limited company which, by virtue of certain common ownership features, is unable to deal at arm's length with other specific limited companies.

7

Audit. *n.* 1. An examination of books of account and supporting evidence to determine the reliability of the information recorded. 2. In connection with financial statements, an examination intended to lead to the expression of an opinion as to whether financial statements of an enterprise present fairly its position as at a given date and the results of its operations for the period ended on that date in accordance with generally accepted accounting principles applied on a basis consistent with that of the preceding year.

Audit. *v.* To conduct an examination of accounts or other records.

Audit programme. The procedures or a detailed listing of the procedures of a particular audit.

Auditing manual. A set of written instructions setting forth the policies and procedures of an auditor for the guidance of his staff.

Auditing procedures. The acts performed in an audit; the techniques of examination, investigation, substantiation, and verification used in the conduct of an audit. (Compare **Auditing standards.**)

Auditing standards. 1. Objectives established for an audit; measure of the quality of performance of auditing procedures; basic principles of auditing which establish the nature and extent of the evidence to be gathered by means of auditing procedures. (Compare **Auditing procedures.**) 2. (*U.S.*) Measure of the quality of an audit conducted by properly trained persons possessing an independent mental attitude, exercising due professional care in the performance of auditing procedures established after an adequate study and evaluation of the existing systems of accounting procedures and internal control and terminating with the report on the financial statements stating that the financial position of the business as at a given date and the results of its operations for the period ended on that date are presented fairly in accordance with generally accepted accounting principles applied on a basis consistent with the preceding period.

Auditor. A person who examines and reports on accounts and records, either in a professional capacity or as an employee.

Auditor's certificate.
Audit certificate. (*obs.*) Term formerly used to describe the auditor's report. It is now rarely used by auditors in the expression of opinion since it seems to imply a degree of certainty more appropriately related to matters of fact solely rather than of fact and opinion.

Auditor's report.
Audit report. 1. The formal document in which the auditor expresses his opinion as to the fairness of the financial statements in accordance with

equal expenses. It is usually expressed as the dollar volume of sales required to cover both fixed and variable expenses. If the amount of fixed expenses and the percentage of variable expenses to sales are known, the sales required to break even may be computed by solving the equation $S = F.E. + aS$, where S = sales to break even, $F.E.$ = amount of fixed expenses, a = percentage of variable expenses to sales.

Break-up value. See **Liquidation value.**

Broker. A middleman or limited agent, often acting for both parties. (Compare **Agent.**)

Budget. 1. A detailed estimate of future transactions, either in terms of quantities, or money values or both, designed to provide a plan for and control over future operations and activities. (Budgets may be fixed or flexible depending on whether the emphasis is placed on only one level of activity or on varying rates of activity.) 2. A portion of a budget or a separate budget dealing with a specific type of transaction, e.g. capital budget relating to proposed additions to fixed assets and their financing, cash budget covering estimated cash receipts and disbursements, and operating budget relating to estimated revenues and expenses.

Budgetary control. The whole process of planning, executing, and evaluating a programme of business activities by the use of a budget.

Bull. *n.* An investor who believes that security or commodity prices are due to rise and buys securities or commodities with this in mind. (Compare **Bear.**)

Burden. See **Factory overhead, Factory service.**

Business. The carrying on of trade or commerce with a view to profit.

Buyers' market. A condition within an industry or geographic area where the supply of a product or service exceeds the demand; hence trading conditions favour the buyer. (Compare **Sellers' market.**)

By-law. 1. A secondary or subordinate law dealing with matters of local or internal regulation. 2. In a business organization, the rules approved by the owners or members to regulate the method of operations of the business.

By-product. A marketable product of lesser importance produced as an incident to the production of a major product. (Compare **Joint products.**)

C

Call. With reference to share capital, a payment requested by the directors on a subscription, or an amount otherwise due under the terms of a subscription agreement.

Call loan. A loan payable on demand at the behest of either the borrower or the lender and to which days of grace are usually not applicable.

Capital. 1. The amount of property owned by an individual or company at a specified time, as distinct from the income received during a given period. In this sense, capital means wealth, i.e. tangible and intangible property and property rights. 2. The interest of the owner or proprietors in the assets of a business. Capital in this sense is often called owners' equity, proprietorship equity, net assets or net worth, and is represented by the excess of the total assets over the total liabilities to outside interests. 3. In a limited company, that portion of the equity contributed by the shareholders which may be returned to the shareholders only after compliance with the formalities imposed by the governing act, the letters patent or the memorandum of association. 4. The total funds provided by lenders (usually restricted to long-term lenders) and by owners for the use of the business. 5. (*executorship and trusteeship accounting*) See **Corpus.**

Capital account. 1. An account for part or all of the owners' equity. Often limited to that portion of the owners' equity that is deemed to be permanent. 2. (*executorship and trusteeship accounting*) The statement of estate corpus. 3. A section of a **Double account form of balance sheet.**

Capital asset. 1. An asset, whether tangible or intangible, intended for long-term use and held as such. See **Fixed asset.** 2. (*governmental accounting*) Any asset of the capital fund.

Capital budget. See **Budget** 2.

Capital cost allowance. An amount allowed, under *The Income Tax Act* (Canada) and Regulations, with respect to certain assets, in computing a taxpayer's income from a business or property for a taxation year. It may differ from the amount charged for the period in depreciation accounting.

Capital expenditure. 1. An outlay or incurrence of a liability to acquire or add to a capital asset. 2. An expenditure yielding more or less enduring benefits.

Capital gain. 1. A profit on the sale of a capital asset. 2. A gain resulting from a scaling down of business debts as in a reorganization, an arrangement with creditors, or a purchase of the company's own bonds at a discount.

Capital loss. Loss on sale or disposition of a capital asset.

Capital stock. 1. The ownership shares of a limited company authorized by its instrument of incorporation. (Compare **Share capital.**) 2. (*Br.*) A

form of corporate capital distinguished from shares in that (a) stock must be fully paid up but shares may be only partly paid up; (b) stock may be transferred in fractional parts but a share cannot be divided; (c) each share retains a distinguishing number but stock does not; and (d) a company cannot issue stock in the first instance but may convert fully paid shares into stock.

Capital surplus. 1. The statutory designation under some Companies Acts to describe earned surplus appropriated in connection with the redemption of preferred shares under certain circumstances. A form of **Reserve**. 2. (*obs.*) Premium on stock issue (should be designated as contributed surplus). 3. (*obs.*) Accumulated capital gains (should be designated as part of earned surplus).

Capitalize. 1. To design or arrange the capital structure of a company. 2. To charge an expenditure to a capital asset account rather than to an expense account. 3. To appropriate (surplus) for permanent retention, e.g. by the issue of a stock dividend.

Carry back. (*income tax*) The right to apply a current loss against the taxable income of a prior period.

Carry forward. (*income tax*) The right to apply a current loss against the taxable income of future periods (usually after the current loss has first been partially used in reducing the taxable income of allowable prior periods).

Carrying charge. 1. A cost of owning property. 2. An addition to the selling price of an article sold on the instalment plan.

Carrying value. See **Book value**.

Cash. 1. Legal tender. 2. Coin or specie, bank notes, money orders, postal notes, cheques and accepted sight drafts believed to be good, and (by extension) the balances in respect of demand and savings deposits at banks or other responsible financial institutions, usually after deduction of any outstanding cheques and other similar items.

Cash audit. An examination of cash transactions for a stated period. A cash audit is detailed in character but limited in scope. It is concerned with the accuracy of the records of cash receipts and disbursements primarily to establish the balance of cash for which the persons charged with responsibility are accountable.

Cash basis of accounting. A method of recording transactions by which revenues and costs are reflected in the accounts in the period in which the related cash receipts or disbursements occur. (Compare **Accrual basis of accounting.**)

Cash book. A book of original entry for recording cash received and paid out. In practice, the cash book is frequently replaced by two separate books, one to record receipts of cash, the other payments.

Cash budget. See **Budget** 2.

Cash discount. A reduction of debt, granted by a creditor in consideration of payment within a prescribed time.

Cash flow statement. See **Statement, Cash flow.**

Cash statement. See **Statement, Cash.**

Cash surrender value. The amount recoverable on the cancellation of some types of life insurance contracts. This is often the limit which the insured can borrow against the contract.

Certified cheque. A cheque guaranteed by the bank on which it is drawn. The bank stamps the face of the cheque to indicate that it has been certified.

Certificate. A document formally attesting a fact.

Charge. *n.* See **Debit.** *n.*

Charge. *v.* See **Debit.** *v.*

Charge and discharge, Statement of. See **Statement of charge and discharge.**

Charge off. *v.* To treat as an expense or a loss an item originally regarded as an asset; to write off.

Chart of accounts. A list of the account numbers and names in a ledger.

Charter. *n.* (*colloq.*) The letters patent, special Act or other legal documents creating a corporation.

Charter. *v.* To lease or hire.

Chattel. Property other than real property; personal property.

Check. *n.* 1. Control or supervision to secure accuracy. 2. (*U.S.*) Cheque.

Check. *v.t.* 1. To compare two or more amounts in different places. 2. To place a mark on an item after verifying it.

Cheque. A bill of exchange drawn on a bank, payable on demand.

Cheque register. A book of original entry in which cheques issued are recorded systematically.

C.I.F. (*abbr.*) Cost, insurance, and freight. The price of goods to be sold includes charges for handling, insurance and freight up to delivery to a foreign port. (Compare **F.A.S.** and **F.O.B.**)

Circularize. To communicate with a group to get their reaction to the contents of the communication; to confirm by correspondence.

Circularization. The act or result of circularizing. See **Confirmation** 2.

Circulating capital. See **Working capital.**

Class. *n.* Generally, a division of things according to quantity or grade. In business, a number of specialized meanings have evolved. 1. (*insurance*) The persons covered by a group life insurance contract. 2. (*income tax*) A group of assets subject to the same rate of capital cost allowance. 3. (*shares*) A division of share capital required when different rights are attached to some shares.

Classification. The allocation or grouping of items in accounts or statements, according to a specific pattern. Expenditures, for example, may be classified by character, e.g. in governmental accounting as current expenses, provision for debt retirement, or capital outlay; by function, e.g. production, distribution, finance, etc.; by activity, e.g. mixing, grinding, shipping, etc.; or by object, e.g. a specific article or service.

Clean surplus. See **All-inclusive income statement.**

Clearing account. An account used as a temporary repository for amounts of a recurring nature which are eventually transferred to other accounts.

Clearing house. An organization that facilitates transfer transactions among members of an industry, profession or other group; e.g. a bank clearing house allows daily settlements to be made among banks for cheques drawn, deposits transferred, etc.

Close. *v.* The act of making closing entries.

Closing entry. An entry made at the end of an accounting period for the purpose of transferring the balances in nominal accounts (revenue, income, expense or loss) to the profit and loss, surplus, capital, or owners' current accounts.

C.O.D. (*abbr.*) Cash on delivery. A condition of sale where the purchaser is required to pay the purchase price in cash immediately on the delivery of the goods or rendering of the service.

Co-insurance. *adj.* A clause in an insurance contract requiring the insured to maintain an agreed percentage of insurance to the value of the thing insured or, failing this, to contribute proportionately to his own loss. The percentages in common use are 80%, 90% and 100%.

Collate. *v.* (*machine accounting*) To arrange two lots of punched cards into a single lot according to a predetermined pattern.

Collateral. That which is pledged for fulfilment of an obligation or debt, e.g. land, buildings, and plant in the case of mortgage bonds; accounts receivable and stock-in-trade for a bank loan, etc.

Combined statement. A composite financial statement comprising the accounts of two or more companies which may or may not be associated. It differs from a consolidated statement in that no adjustment is made to eliminate one company's investment, if any, in the capital of another. (Compare **Consolidate** 1.)

Commitment. 1. An undertaking; an informal, or formal, guarantee. 2. See **Encumbrance** 1.

Common-size statement. See **Statement, Common-size.**

Common stock. A class of share capital; the class representing the residual equity in the assets and earnings of a business.

Company. Any association, whether incorporated or unincorporated, of persons who are joined in a common interest, generally for the purpose of carrying on a business undertaking. (Compare **Corporation, Limited company.**)

Comparable. 1. Able to be compared. 2. Worthy of being compared.

Comparative statement. A form of financial statement presentation in which current amounts and corresponding amounts from previous periods are set out. In connection with annual financial statements, the usual practice is to set out the previous year's figures alongside those of the current year.

Compare. 1. To represent as similar. 2. To set out similarities and differences. 3. (*auditing*) To verify the similarity of amounts which appear in different locations.

Composite life depreciation. See **Depreciation unit.**

Compromise. *n.* See **Arrangement** 2.

Comptroller. A general term applied to an officer or senior employee of a business whose responsibilities generally involve the accounting control functions of the business.

Confirmation. 1. Corroboration or verification. 2. (*auditing*) Verification from sources other than the books and records under review, usually by correspondence with a third party, particularly with respect to: (a) amounts owing to the client, e.g. accounts receivable, (b) liabilities of the client, e.g. bank loans, (c) the existence, condition or value of assets in the possession and control of persons other than the client, e.g. securities held for safekeeping by a bank. The confirmation is known as positive if the third party is requested to reply in any event, and as negative if a reply requested only in the case of disagreement.

Conservatism. A point of view which, in the absence of a clear-cut choice, prefers to apply an accounting practice that tends to produce lower values for assets and profits than would the application of another acceptable practice.

Consignment. A shipment of goods made under an agreement whereby the receiver (the consignee) undertakes to sell or otherwise dispose of the goods as agent on behalf of the shipper (the consignor). The latter retains title to the goods until they are sold or disposed of according to the arrangement.

Consistency. The uniform application of accounting principles in the preparation and presentation of financial statements, particularly as to account classifications, bases of valuation and methods of accrual. This constant adherence to uniform accounting principles can be applied to different statements bearing the same date (sometimes called "horizontal" consistency) and to the financial statements of the same organization for different accounting periods (sometimes called "vertical" consistency).

Consolidate. 1. To combine the financial statements of a parent company and one or more of its subsidiaries so as to ignore the separate legal identity of the consolidated companies and present the financial position and operating results of the group as one economic unit. (Compare **Combined statement.**) 2. To bring together.

Consolidated balance sheet. A balance sheet in which the assets and liabilities of subsidiary companies have been combined with those of the parent company after eliminating inter-company debts, inter-company profits, and inter-company investments. It is a special form of balance sheet showing the financial position of the parent company and the consolidated subsidiaries viewed as a single economic unit.

Consolidated earned surplus. The earned surplus shown in a consolidated balance sheet. It consists broadly of the combined earned surpluses of the companies whose accounts have been consolidated less: (1) the minority shareholders' interest therein, (2) the interest of the parent company in the surplus of consolidated subsidiaries at the respective dates of acquisition, and (3) unrealized inter-company profits.

Consolidated statement of profit and loss. An income statement in which the revenues and expenses of a parent company have been combined with those of some or all of its subsidiaries after eliminating the effect of inter-company transactions.

Contingency fund. Cash or investments set aside or reserved for undetermined expenditures.

Contingency reserve. See **Reserve** 1.

19

Contingent asset. Something of potential value depending on the occurrence or non-occurrence of some specific future event. The face value of an insurance policy is a contingent asset to the beneficiary.

Contingent liability. A legal obligation that may arise out of present circumstances provided certain developments occur. The possibility of a future liability does not of itself constitute a contingent liability; it must be a possibility arising out of present circumstances or pending affairs.

Continuous audit. Any audit of which detailed portions are performed continuously or at short intervals during the accounting period.

Contra. 1. Off-setting, e.g. a contra account. 2. On the opposite side of an account or statement, e.g. assets held in trust are shown on one side of a balance sheet and the liability in respect of the trust is shown "contra".

Contra account. An account that wholly or partially offsets another account, e.g. mutual claims against each other by two persons.

Contract. *n.* An engagement or agreement between competent parties upon a legal consideration to do or abstain from doing something. Requirements of a binding contract are: an offer and its acceptance; form or consideration; capacity of the parties to make a contract; genuine consent; legality of the objects of the contract.

Contributed surplus. 1. Surplus contributed by shareholders being the portion of the equity of shareholders that represents the premium received on the issue of par value shares, the portion of proceeds of issue of no par value shares that has been allocated to surplus, the proceeds of sale of donated shares, profit on forfeited shares, credits resulting from redemption or conversion of shares at less than the amount set up as share capital, or any other contributions in excess of par or stated value of shares made by shareholders as such. 2. Capital donations from other sources, e.g. government subsidies, donation of land sites.

Control. *n.* 1. The power to influence actions (e.g. a controlling interest in a limited company is possessed by anyone, or any group, being able to select the majority of the company's directors). 2. The accounting procedures used as a check on the reliability of the information contained in accounting records (e.g. the use of a control to balance the total of the accounts in a subsidiary ledger). Part of a system of internal control.

Controller. See **Comptroller.**

Control(ling) account. A general ledger account, the balance of which represents the total of the balances of the accounts in a subsidiary ledger, e.g. the accounts receivable ledger.

Controlling interest. See **Control** 1.

Convention. A generally accepted assumption, rule, or practice.

Convertible. A feature attached to some securities, usually bonds and shares, permitting the owners to turn the securities into another class of security in accordance with conditions specified in the original securities.

Co-operative. *n.* An incorporated organization formed for the benefit of its members (owners) with certain economic characteristics, viz.: a limited return on invested capital; the payment of patronage returns, or dividends, to its producers and/or customers, possibly at different rates for different classes of business, possibly only to members; the setting aside of funds in reserves as decided by its directors. Control is exercised by the members usually on the basis of one vote per member. There are also important distinguishing social characteristics.

Copyright. *n.* The exclusive right, conferred by *The Copyright Act* (Canada), to produce or reproduce an original literary, dramatic, musical or artistic work. In general, the term of copyright protection is for the life of the author and fifty years after his death, but it is usual to amortize the cost of a copyright purchased over a much shorter period.

Corporation. Any legal entity constituting a body corporate as determined by statute, either with or without share capital. (Compare **Company, Limited company.**)

Corpus. The principal or capital of an estate, as opposed to the income.

Correcting entry. An entry made for the purpose of rectifying an error in the books of account.

Cost. The amount, measured in money, of the expenditure to obtain goods or services. See **Expired cost, Unexpired cost.** (Compare **Expense, Loss.**)

Cost accounting. That branch of accounting concerned with the classification, recording, analysis, and interpretation of expenditures associated with the production and distribution of goods and services.

Cost centre. A unit, group, or subdivision of industrial organization, used to segregate and distribute the factory expenses.

Cost ledger. A subsidiary ledger containing accounts relating exclusively to cost accounting.

Cost and market, Lower of. See **Lower of cost and market.**

Cost sheet. A summary of all of the cost elements of a particular product or service.

Coverage. The nature and amount of risk insured in an insurance contract.

Credit. *n.* 1. The ability to buy or borrow in consideration of a promise to pay at a later date. 2. An entry reflecting the creation of or addition to a liability, or owners' equity, or revenue, or the reduction or elimination of an asset or expense; an entry on the right-hand side of an account. (Converse of **Debit.**)

Credit. *v.* To record a credit entry in books of account.

Creditor. One to whom a debt is owed.

Credit Union. A non-profit co-operative organization designed to encourage saving by its members and to make small loans to its members; usually regulated by provincial statute.

Cremation certificate. A sworn statement by a trustee or other agent that (matured or redeemed) securities listed in the statement have been destroyed.

Cum div. or **Cum dividend.** The condition of shares whose quoted market or sale price includes a declared dividend. This condition pertains between the declaration date of the dividend and the record date. (Compare **Ex div.** or **Ex dividend.**)

Cumulative shares. Shares of a limited company which contain a right to a specified annual dividend before any dividend can be paid on junior classes of shares.

Current account. A running account with a person or organization. A bank current account is usually a chequing account as contrasted with a savings account; a partner's current account is a record of his drawings and his portion of profits available for withdrawal, as contrasted with his permanent investment in the business which is reflected in his capital account. (Compare **Account current.**)

Current asset. An asset that, in the normal course of operations, is expected to be converted into cash or consumed in the production of income within one year or within the normal operating cycle where that is longer than a year. An asset subject to restrictions that prevent its use for current operating purposes should not be included as a current asset.

Current liability. A debt owing which will fall due within one year. A liability payable within one year but for which provision has been made for payment from other than current resources may properly be excluded.

Current operating concept. A method of statement presentation where unusual and non-recurring operating items which occurred in the accounting period are shown in the statement of surplus rather than in the statement of profit and loss. (Compare **Clean surplus.**)

Current ratio. The arithmetical relationship between current assets and liabilities, used as a measure of liquidity. It is usually stated as a number representing the amount of current assets expressed as a multiple of the amount of current liabilities, e.g. with current assets of $510,000 and current liabilities of $200,000 the current ratio is 2.55:1, or 2.55. (Compare **Acid test ratio.**)

Cut-off. *n.* The proper segregation of income and expense items between one accounting period and the next.

Cycle billing. A method of sending statements to customers where groups of customers are billed throughout the period so that all customers are billed once in each period. This method is in contrast to billing all customers as at the end of the period.

D

Day book. A chronological record of the transactions of an enterprise, particularly transactions relating to merchandise. Day books have largely been supplanted by copies of invoices, cash register tapes, etc.

Debenture. A certificate of indebtedness issued by a government or company, generally being one of a number of such certificates. The term usually implies an unsecured obligation. (Compare **Bond.**)

Debit. *n.* An entry on the left-hand side of an account, recording the creation of, or addition to, an asset, the incurring of an expense, or the reduction or elimination of a liability, owners' equity or revenue; a **charge.** (Converse of **Credit** 2.)

Debit. *v.* To record a debit entry in books of account.

Debt. Money, goods, or services owing by one person (the debtor), to another (the creditor) payable either at the present or at some future time.

Declaration. 1. The formal act of a board of directors of a limited company which creates a liability for a dividend. See **Dividend** 1. 2. Any formal document attesting a fact. 3. The formal statement of facts, given by the insured to the insurer, upon which the risk in the underwriting of the insurance contract is based.

Declaration date. The date on which the board of directors of a limited company declares a dividend.

Deferment.

Deferral. An item of revenue received or receivable or expense incurred but applicable to a subsequent period, and accordingly carried forward on the balance sheet for disposition in a future period. See **Deferred charge, Deferred credit, Deferred revenue.**

Deferred charge. 1. A long-term expense prepayment; an expenditure, other than a capital expenditure, the benefit of which will extend over a period of years from the time of incurrence and meanwhile is carried forward to be assigned to expense over a period of years. (Compare **Prepaid expense** 1.) 2. Balance of amounts paid for goods or services received for which the payee has no further obligation and meanwhile is carried forward to be assigned to expense in future years (Compare **Prepaid expense** 2.)

Deferred credit. 1. An amount received, recorded as receivable or, as in deferred income taxes, provided for that represents a reduction of future expenses. 2. See **Deferred revenue.**

Deferred liability. See **Long-term liability.**

Deferred revenue. An amount of revenue received or recorded as receivable but not yet earned.

Deferred tax credit. The deferment of income tax otherwise payable resulting from the use of significantly larger deductions in calculating taxable income than those used in calculating the net income or profit shown in the taxpayer's financial statements. The deductions in computing taxable income are proper and arise from different amounts being allowed by the taxing authorities than are deducted in accordance with sound accounting practices.

Deficiency. A failure to satisfy or a falling short of some requirement. In accounting, the term should not be used without qualifying words indicating the nature of the deficiency, e.g. a deficiency to creditors.

Deficiency account. A statement of an insolvent debtor which accounts for the excess of liabilities over the estimated realizable value of the assets; also, the ledger account showing the deficiency of assets upon realization and liquidation.

Deficit. The amount by which the total assets of an incorporated enterprise, as shown by the books, fall short of the total of liabilities, plus share capital and contributed surplus, if any. (Converse of **Surplus.**) In a sole proprietorship or a partnership, an excess of liabilities (not including owners' capital) over assets is sometimes called a deficit.

Demand loan. See **Call loan.**

Demurrage. A charge made by the carrier for a delay in loading or unloading a vessel (including a ship, railway car or other vehicles) beyond the time allowed.

Denial. (*auditing*) The report by an auditor setting out the fact that, for stated reasons which arose from his audit, he is unable to express an opinion on the financial statements of his client.

Department. A separate division of a business, especially for accounting and administrative purposes.

Depletion. 1. A reduction in quantity of wasting assets, as a result of consumption or removal of natural resources, e.g. standing timber, mineral deposits. 2. An allowance made in the accounts to reflect the cost of the portion of wasting assets consumed or removed.

Deposit. A lodging of cash, securities, etc. with others. A bank deposit is a payment made into a bank for subsequent withdrawal or to apply on an overdraft.

Depreciation. 1. The gradual exhaustion of the service capacity of fixed assets which is not restored by maintenance practices. It is the consequence of such factors as use, obsolescence, inadequacy, and decay. 2. A proportionate charge as an expense to an accounting period based on the cost or other recorded value of fixed assets. See **Depreciation accounting.**

Depreciation accounting. An accounting procedure in which the cost or other recorded value of a fixed asset less estimated salvage (if any) is distributed over its estimated useful life in a systematic and rational manner. It is a process of allocation, not valuation. (Compare **Renewal accounting, Retirement accounting.**)

Depreciation method. Any method calculating depreciation expense for the accounting period. The most frequently used methods are: (a) *Straight line method* in which the periodic charge is computed by dividing the cost or other value of the asset by the estimated number of periods of service life. (b) *Diminishing balance method* in which the periodic charge is computed as a constant proportion of the asset's net book value (cost or other book value less depreciation already charged). (c) *Sum of the years' digits* method in which the original depreciable value of the asset is allocated to the individual years on a reducing basis by multiplying the depreciable value by a fraction in which the numerator is the number of years of estimated life remaining (including the year for which depreciation is being computed), and the denominator is the sum of the series of numbers representing the successive years in the total estimated life. For an asset having an estimated life of five years, the denominator is 15 (i.e. $1 + 2 + 3 + 4 + 5$), and the numerator for the first year is 5, for the second year 4, and so on. (d) *Production or service-output method* in which the periodic charge is that proportion of the total depreciation over the life of the asset that the production or use during the period bears to the total estimated production or use to be obtained from the asset. (e) *Sinking fund method* in which the periodic charge is computed as the periodic amount which, together with interest at a specified rate compounded annually on the accumulated amount, will accumulate to the original cost or other recorded value of the fixed asset by the estimated date of retirement.

Depreciation rate. A percentage which when applied to the cost or other recorded value of the depreciation unit will produce the depreciation expense for the period applicable to the asset or group of assets.

Depreciation unit. The asset or asset group to which a depreciation rate is applied. (a) *Group or composite life.* A method of accounting for depreciation which deals with a group of assets rather than with single fixed assets. When an asset is retired, the cost of the asset, after reduction by any salvage value, is written off against the accumulated depreciation. The method assumes that the estimate of average life will be such that the over-depreciation of some assets will be balanced by the under-depreciation of others in the group. (b) *Unit or item.* A method of accounting for depreciation which deals with single fixed assets rather than with groups. When the individual asset is retired, the loss or gain is recognized as such.

Development costs.
Development expense. 1. Expenditures made to bring a mineral property or other natural resources into production, but usually not including exploration or equipment costs. 2. Expenditures made in promoting a new product or enterprise.

Differential cost. The amount by which the total costs are increased by the last unit of output at any given volume of production.

Diminishing balance method. See Depreciation method.

Direct cost. 1. An item of cost that may reasonably and conveniently be identified with a specific unit of product or with a specific operation, process, department, or other cost unit. 2. (*colloq.*) See **Differential cost.**

Direct costing. A costing method in which only direct materials, direct labour and variable overhead are charged to inventory. All fixed manufacturing expense such as depreciation, insurance, factory and property taxes, salaries of supervisors, foremen and factory maintenance staff are excluded from the inventory valuation.

Direct labour. The cost of labour expended immediately upon the direct materials that will comprise the finished product of a manufacturing process. (Compare **Indirect labour.**)

Direct material. The cost of material that will form an integral part of the final product of a manufacturing process. (Compare **Indirect material, Raw material.**)

Disbursement. A payment out in cash or by cheque. (Compare **Expenditure.**)

Disclaimer (*auditing*) A written declaration attached to financial statements prepared by, or with the assistance of, a public accountant setting out that, since the terms of the engagement did not require an audit to be made, he is not in a position to express an opinion on the financial statements.

Discount. *n.* 1. A reduction from a list price or stated amount. 2. The amount by which the selling price of a bond or the issue price of a share is less than the par value. 3. The amount deducted, as interest in advance, from the maturity value of a note when it is sold to a bank for its present worth, usually with a guarantee; or any similar difference between present worth and value at maturity.

Discount. *v.* To sell for its present worth, either with or without recourse, a note or other claim or right to future value.

Distributable surplus. 1. (*legal*) As required by some Companies Acts, any portion of the proceeds of the issue of shares without par value not allocated to share capital. A form of **contributed surplus.** 2. (*colloq.*) See **Earned surplus—unappropriated.**

Dividend. 1. An amount designated for distribution to the shareholders of a limited company in proportion to their holdings of shares of the company, having due regard for the respective rights of various classes of shares. 2. An amount distributed to the shareholders of a limited company upon the liquidation of the compay. 3. An amount distributed to the creditors, *pro rata,* out of the net amount realized in a bankrupt estate. 4. A patronage return to the customers or members of a co-operative.

Dividend payable. A dividend which has been declared but not yet paid.

Donated surplus. Surplus resulting from contributions of assets, with no consideration, from shareholders and others; a form of **contributed surplus.**

Double account form of balance sheet.
Double account system. See **Balance sheet, Form of.**

Double entry bookkeeping. The system of bookkeeping, now in general use, in which every transaction is recorded in one or more accounts as a debit and in one or more as a credit in such a manner that the total of the debit entries equals the total of the credit entries. Double entry bookkeeping may be said to rest upon the twofold aspect of every transaction representing an exchange of values, i.e. a value given and a value received, or upon the twofold aspect of everything of value, namely the valuable possession itself and the equities or personal claims against such value. (Compare **Single entry bookkeeping.**)

Doubtful account.
Doubtful debt. An account or note receivable, the ultimate collectibility of which is uncertain. (Compare **Bad debt.**)

Down time. Time lost from the use of machinery and equipment due to necessary repairs, retooling or programming.

Draft. See **Bill of exchange.**

Drawings. Withdrawals of assets (usually cash or merchandise) from a business by a sole proprietor or partner.

E

E. & O. E. (*abbr.*) Errors and omissions excepted. Sometimes put on an invoice or statement of account to reserve the right to make corrections if errors are subsequently found.

Earn To deserve or have the right to income or revenue.

Earned income. 1. See **Realized income.** 2. (*income tax*) Generally income from personal services and rentals. The precise meaning of the term is dependent upon the taxing statute and interpretation thereof.

Earned surplus. The net accumulation, after deducting dividends, of profits less losses arising from the operations of the business. Synonymous terms which are more descriptive of the source of this balance include: retained earnings, undistributed profits, accumulated earnings, earnings retained (or reinvested) in the business. There are two divisions: (a) *Appropriated.* That portion which has been transferred to a reserve. See **Reserve.** (b) *Unappropriated.* That portion which has not been transferred to a reserve and is thus, in the absence of any restrictions, available for dividends.

Earning power. The ability of an enterprise or security to earn. The term is usually applied to the present value of estimated future earnings.

Earnings. 1. A generic term used to mean income or profit. 2. (*colloq.*) Revenue.

Earnings per share. The proportion of the profit or income for the period attributable to a share of the issued capital of a limited company. In arriving at this figure extraordinary gains and losses, such as a substantial loss or gain on the disposal of fixed assets or investments, are usually deleted from the computation of profit for the period in order that the remaining figure be comparable with the figures computed in the same way for other periods.

Economic life. The period during which a fixed asset can efficiently be kept in use, as opposed to its physical life which ignores obsolescence and excessive maintenance costs. (Compare **Useful life.**)

Effective rate. The ratio of income realized to the sum invested. (Compare **Nominal rate.**)

Efficiency variance. The difference between the standard cost of direct labour and overhead and actual cost resulting from causes other than changes in price.

Electronic data processing. The use of electronic equipment, usually including electronic computers, in the assembling, classifying, recording, analyzing, and reporting of information.

Eliminating entries. Adjustments in the preparation of consolidated financial statements, or group accounts, made to prevent duplication due to intercompany transactions.

Encumbrance. 1. An expenditure commitment charged against a budget appropriation (chiefly in governmental accounting). 2. A charge upon real or personal property.

Endowment fund. Property (often in the form of cash or investments acquired by gift or bequest) of a charitable, religious, educational, or other non-profit institution, the income from which is used for general or specific purposes according to the conditions attaching to the gifts, and the principal of which must be maintained intact or applied to the purposes of the gift.

Enterprise. A company or sole proprietorship.

Entity accounting. Accounting for a branch, department, or company without regard to its association with, control by, or succession from, another organization.

Entity concept. The view that a business should be considered apart from its owners. Thus, (a) the income of any business entity is considered to accrue to the business rather than to the owners, and (b) the accounts of the business should reflect the resources entrusted to the business entity and the equitable and legal interests in these resources.

Entry. A record, in a book of account or other accounting document, of the effect of an operation or transaction.

Equity. 1. The claim or right of proprietors or creditors to the assets of a business. 2. (*colloq.*) The residual interest of an owner or shareholder.

Escrow. An agreement whereby a deed, money or other property is deposited with a trustee to be held until certain conditions are fulfilled.

Examine. To audit, investigate, or probe.

Exception. See **Qualification.**

Exchange. *n.* 1. The charge made by a bank for handling a bill of exchange drawn on another bank or on a branch of the same bank in another location. 2. See **Foreign exchange.** 3. An organized market for the purchase and sale of stocks or commodities.

Exclusion. A limitation in the coverage of an insurance contract.

Ex div. or **Ex dividend.** The condition of shares whose quoted market price does not include a declared dividend. This condition pertains after the record date and before the payment date of the dividend. (Compare **Cum div.** or **Cum dividend.**)

Executor. A person appointed by a testator to give effect to his will after his death. (Compare **Administrator 2.**)

Exhibit. A part of a financial statement; sometimes the principal statements are called exhibits while the supplementary statements are called schedules.

Expenditure. A disbursement, a liability incurred, or the transfer of property for the purpose of obtaining goods or services. Some expenditures are not or do not become expenses, e.g. purchase of securities. (Compare **Disbursement, Expense.**)

Expense. 1. A cost incurred in the process of earning the revenue attributed to a period, including those costs not assignable to any particular revenue but incurred during the period in the course of ordinary operations and not assignable to the operations of a future period or periods. (Compare **Cost, Expenditure, Loss.**) 2. (*colloq.*) A general term applied to the costs of carrying on business.

Expired cost. 1. An expenditure whose benefit has been exhausted; an expense. (Compare **Unexpired cost.**) 2. Sometimes used with respect to an expenditure without return or benefit; a loss. (Compare **Unexpired cost.**)

Ex rights. The condition of shares (sometimes also of bonds) whose quoted market price does not include the right, formerly attached to the shares, to purchase new shares, the rights having expired or been retained by the vendor.

Extend. 1. To multiply. 2. To widen or enlarge (e.g. to extend the scope of an audit).

30

External auditor. 1. Any auditor not an employee of the enterprise under review. (Compare **Internal auditor.**) 2. An auditor appointed for a company in accordance with the requirements of the governing Companies Act or other statute; a shareholders' auditor. (Compare **Internal auditor.**)

F

Face amount.
Face value. See **Par value.**

Factor. *n.* 1. An agent; commonly used to describe an individual or company that buys receivables at a discount from another to provide the vendor with cash and/or to relieve the vendor of the risk of collecting the receivables. 2. (*math.*) Any of the numbers which, when multiplied together, form a product. 3. A circumstance, influence or fact that produces a result.

Factory ledger. A subsidiary ledger in which manufacturing costs are assembled; a goods-in-process ledger.

Factory overhead.
Factory service. All production costs other than direct material and direct labour costs. These terms include all costs necessary to the operation and maintenance of the plant including wages of foremen, building and machinery upkeep, depreciation, light, heating, repairs, insurance, taxes, etc.

Factory supplies. Indirect materials; goods which are used in the manufacturing process, but which do not form part of the material content of the finished product or which do not do so in conveniently measurable quantity or form.

Fair market value. The value determined by "bona fide" bargaining between well-informed independent buyers and sellers; an estimate of such value in the absence of actual transactions.

F.A.S. (*abbr.*) Free alongside; the price of goods to be sold includes all charges until the goods are placed alongside the vessel (including a ship, railway car or other vehicle) in which they are to be shipped. (Compare **C.I.F.** and **F.O.B.**)

Field. *n.* (*machine accounting*) A group of one or more characters treated as a unit in a mechanized or electronic data processing system.

Fifo. See **First in, first out.**

Financial condition.
Financial position. The state of affairs represented by the assets, liabilities, and owners' equity at any specified time.

Financial expense. The classification for financial statement purposes of those expenses of an organization relating to the cost of financing its operations; as opposed to those expenses incurred for other specialized functions, such as manufacturing, administration or selling.

Financial statement. 1. A balance sheet, statement of profit and loss, statement of receipts and disbursements, statement of source and application of funds, or any other formal accounting report. 2. A report comprising several accounting statements such as those mentioned in 1.

Finished goods.
Finished stock. Goods which have been manufactured or processed and are ready for sale or other disposition.

First in, first out ("Fifo"). A method of allocating costs of materials or goods to production or cost of sales and to inventory, in which the cost of goods chargeable to current production or cost of sales is computed as though the goods were used or sold in order of their acquisition.

Fiscal period. The period for which financial statements are regularly prepared, generally a twelve-month period but not necessarily the calendar year. (Compare **Natural business year.**)

Fixed asset. A tangible long-term asset, such as land, building, equipment, etc., held for use rather than for sale.

Fixed budget. See **Budget 1.**

Fixed cost.

Fixed expense. An expense that remains relatively unchanged in total regardless of the volume of business or within a fairly wide range of volume. (Compare **Semi-variable cost, Semi-variable expense, Variable cost, Variable expense.**)

Fixture. A part of fixed assets usually consisting of machinery or equipment attached to or forming a normal part of a building.

Flat. (*colloq.*) Nil, particularly as to the balance of an account and, in the case of bonds, without accrued interest.

Flexible budget. See **Budget 1.**

Flow chart. A graphic presentation of the movement of goods, documents or work, especially related to the operations of a business.

F.O.B. (*abbr.*) Free on board; the price of goods to be sold includes all charges until the goods are placed aboard the vessel (including a ship, railway car or other vehicles) in which they are to be shipped. (Compare **C.I.F.** and **F.A.S.**)

Folio. 1. A sheet of paper folded once; hence, two opposite pages in a book which bear the same number, as in records running across the width of the two pages. 2. The number of a page or of two facing pages which bear the same number.

Foot. *v.* To add.

Foreign business corporation. 1. A corporation created under the laws of another country. 2. (*income tax*) A corporation incorporated in Canada, but which carries on business operations outside of Canada, and has its assets situated outside of Canada. The precise meaning of the term is dependent upon the taxing statute and interpretation thereof.

Foreign exchange. 1. The method by which settlement is made for transactions between countries in lieu of actual shipment of gold. 2. (*colloq.*) The currency of a foreign country. 3. See **Rate of exchange.**

Fraud. A deliberate act of deception or manipulation with the specific intent of cheating or injuring another person or organization and providing illegitimate personal gains.

Freight-in. Freight paid by the purchaser on incoming shipments of goods and materials.

Freight-out. Freight paid or allowed by the seller on shipments of goods and materials to customers.

Functional accounting. The segregation of business transactions by functions or activity.

Fund. 1. A self-balancing accounting entity set up to show capital or trust monies received for specific purpose(s), the income thereon, expenditures for the purpose(s) designated and the assets held against the capital of the fund. See **Fund accounting.** 2. Assets (cash, investments, etc.) set aside for specific purposes. 3. A portion of capital or equity earmarked or designated for specific purposes or for specific interests. Used especially in life insurance accounting, e.g. participating policyholders' fund, shareholders' fund.

Fund accounting. Accounting procedures in which a self-balancing group of accounts is provided for each accounting entity established by legal, contractual, or voluntary action, especially in governmental units. In fund accounting for municipalities, for example, it is customary to account separately for the capital fund, the current, revenue, or general fund, the sinking fund, and sometimes other funds. The accounts for each such entity will record the fund's resources on the one hand and the liabilities, surplus and other credits on the other hand.

Funded debt. See **Long-term liability.**

33

Funds. (*pl.*) Working capital (as used in the expression "Source and Application of Funds").

Futures. The price at which commodities are traded on an organized exchange for future delivery. The price is determined partly by the current price for immediate delivery and partly by the buyer's and seller's estimate of market conditions at the time of future delivery.

G

Gain. A monetary benefit, profit or advantage resulting from a transaction or group of transactions. See **Profit.**

Gang punch. *v.* (*machine accounting*) To punch information from a master card into detail cards, either manually or automatically.

General accounting. That branch of accounting concerned with the principles, classification, recording, analysis and interpretation of the overall financial position and operating results of a business.

General expenses. Expenses not otherwise classified.

General journal. The book of original entry in which are recorded those transactions and adjustments for which specialized journals have not been provided.

General ledger. A ledger comprising all asset, liability, proprietorship, revenue, and expense accounts, in the form of detailed, summary, or controlling accounts or a mixture of these.

Generally accepted. *adj.* Given recognition: on a formal basis, by pronouncements by authoritative sources or organizations; on an informal basis, by usage.

Going concern concept. The view that the business will continue in operation indefinitely, and accordingly that accounting measurements need not necessarily reflect estimated or known liquidation or forced sale values; this concept is of significance especially in the accounting treatment of fixed and intangible assets.

Going concern value.
Going value. 1. The value of an asset or of the net assets based on the assumption of continued use in the operations of the business; as distinct from market or liquidation value. (Compare **Liquidation value.**) 2. (*colloq.*) Capitalized earning power.

Goods. Commodities; tangible assets.

Goods in process. See **Work in process.**

Goodwill. An intangible asset of a business when the business has value in excess of the sum of its net assets. Goodwill has had a variety of definitions, some relating to the nature of the asset, others to its value. As to its nature, it has been said to fall into the three classes of commercial, industrial, and financial goodwill, which are the consequence of favourable attitudes on the part of customers, employees, and creditors, respectively. As to its value, the most common explanations emphasize the present value of expected future earnings in excess of the return required to induce investment.

Governmental accounting. That branch of accounting concerned with the principles, classification, recording, analysis and interpretation of the overall financial position and operating results of municipal, provincial, national and other governmental units.

Gross. *adj.* The total without deductions, e.g. gross sales, gross revenue.

Gross margin.
Gross profit. The margin between cost and selling price; the excess of net sales over the cost of goods sold (and sometimes of inventory losses).

Gross profit test. A test or check on the validity of the closing inventory figure(s) by comparing the rate of gross profit for the period with those of prior periods taking into consideration known changes in selling prices and costs of production.

Group accounts. (*Br.*) The financial statements covering the business of a holding company and its subsidiary companies; the "group accounts" take the form of one or several sets of consolidated statements or a set consisting of the financial statement of each company in the group.

Group depreciation. See Depreciation unit.

Guarantee. *n.* A contract to perform the obligation or discharge the liability of a third person if the latter fails to do so. (Compare **Warranty.**)

Guarantor. One who promises to make good if another fails to pay or otherwise fulfil a contractual obligation. See **Accommodation party.**

H

Hash total. (*machine accounting*) A sum formed for audit or control purposes by adding together fields not normally related by unit of measure (e.g. total of employee's numbers in a payroll).

Hedge. *v.* To buy or sell futures on commodity exchanges for the specific purpose of eliminating or restricting the risk involved in price fluctuations.

Hidden reserve. See Secret reserve.

Historic cost. The total expenditures made by the present owner to acquire title to or exclusive use of an asset.

Holdback. A portion of the progress payments called for under the terms of a contract which is not payable until the contract has been completed.

Holding company. A company engaged principally in holding a controlling interest in the shares of one or more other companies.

Hypothecate. To give collateral.

Idle capacity. Production facilities temporarily idle because of lack of orders, errors in planning, or similar causes.

Idle time. Time lost by labour or machinery because of lack of business, material shortages, machine breakdowns, faulty supervision and similar

Impairment. A reduction or diminution in value.

Imprest fund. A fund kept under the **imprest system,** e.g. imprest petty cash fund.

Imprest system. A system for handling disbursements wherein a specified amount of cash or a bank balance is entrusted to an individual or individuals. The cash or bank balance is reimbursed from time to time for the exact amount of the disbursements on the basis of the vouchers covering the disbursements. At any time, the cash on hand or the bank balance plus the disbursement vouchers not reimbursed should equal the amount of the fund.

Improvement. An expenditure made for the purpose of enhancing the utility of a fixed asset and which may be regarded as an addition to the cost of the property. (Compare **Maintenance, Repair.**)
causes.

Imputed cost. 1. The portion of the total cost of items of goods and services acquired in a lot or produced jointly that is allocated to the individual unit of goods or services. 2. See **Opportunity cost.**

Income. 1. Net profit on business operations for a period. See **Profit** 1. (Compare **Revenue** 1.) 2. Revenue derived from investments and from incidental sources. 3. Revenue of an individual such as salary, interest, rent, etc.

Income account. 1. An account (See **Account** 1.) for a specified class of revenue. 2. See **Profit and loss account.**

Income bond. A bond on which the payment of interest is contingent upon earnings.

Income statement.

Income, statement of. See **Statement of profit and loss.**

Incorporated company. A limited company.

Incremental cost. See **Differential cost.**

Incur. To bear, sustain, become liable for.

Indemnity. Security or protection against the possibility of loss.

Independence. A quality which permits an individual to apply unbiased judgment and objective consideration to established facts in arriving at an opinion or decision.

Indirect cost. See **Overhead.**

Indirect labour. The cost of labour expended which does not directly affect the construction or composition of the finished product of a manufacturing process. (Compare **Direct labour.**)

Indirect liability. See **Contingent liability.**

Indirect material. The cost of material that is necessary to the production of a manufacturing company's goods for sale but does not form part of the final product. (Compare **Direct material.**)

Inner reserve. See **Secret reserve.**

Input. The form of and information on the source data introduced into a data processing system.

Insolvency. The condition of an individual or company unable to discharge its liabilities either because liabilities exceed the realizable value of its assets or because of inability to pay debts as they mature. (Compare **Bankruptcy.**)

Instalment. 1. A partial payment of a debt. 2. Any portion of a debt divided into portions that are made payable at different times.

Instalment sale. A sale in which the price is settled by a series of payments over a period of time.

Insurable interest. (*legal*) An individual's or company's interest or claim on property or service of such a nature that the individual or company would suffer a pecuniary loss as the immediate result of the damage or destruction of such property or service.

Insurance fund. A fund of cash or investments set aside as a measure of self-insurance against loss by fire or other casualty.

Intangible assets. Long-term or non-current assets that lack physical substance, e.g. goodwill, patents, copyrights, trademarks, leaseholds, mineral rights.

Integrated data processing. The coordination or combination of various methods of recording, classifying, and otherwise handling information by mechanical means, e.g. the production of punched cards by typewriter or accounting machine as an adjunct to the original record, with further use of the cards in a computer or tabulating machine.

Inter-company eliminations. See **Eliminating entries.**

Interims.

Interim certificates. Provisional certificates of shares, bonds, or other securities issued pending preparation of formal certificates or payment in full on instalment issues.

Interim report.

Interim statement. A report or statement prepared as at any date or for a period ending on any date within the regular fiscal year.

Internal audit. An audit of an enterprise by an employee or employees of the enterprise; an important element of internal control.

Internal auditor. An employee of an enterprise whose duty it is to audit all or part of the accounts of the enterprise but not to express an opinion on the annual financial statements. (Compare **External auditor.**)

Internal check. A system of allocation of responsibility, division of work and methods of recording transactions whereby the work of an employee or group of employees is checked continuously by having to be in agreement with the work of others or by being dependent upon or otherwise correlated with the work of other employees. An essential feature is that no one employee or group of employees has exclusive control over any transaction or group of transactions. Internal check should not be confused with internal control of which internal check is an important element.

Internal control. The plan of organization and all the coordinated methods and measures adopted within a business to safeguard its assets, ensure the accuracy and reliability of the accounting data, promote operational efficiency and maintain adherence to prescribed policies. The concept of internal control encompasses internal administrative control, internal accounting control, internal audit and internal check.

Interpret. (*machine accounting*) To print information on the same card on which it is punched.

Inter-vivos trust. (*legal*) The right to the use of or benefits from property whose legal ownership has been vested by a living person in a third party.

Intestate. The condition of a deceased who did not leave a will.

Inventory. An itemized list of goods; the annual or other periodic account of stock taken in a business; the articles that are inventoried. In accounting terminology, the word is usually restricted to designate items of tangible personal property which are held for sale in the ordinary course of business, or are in the process of production for such sale, or are to be currently consumed in the production of goods or services to be available for sale.

Inventory certificate. A letter of representation obtained by the auditor from the client or his official, covering the method of taking inventory, the basis of valuation and the ownership of goods included in the inventory. The letter is usually signed by two or more responsible officials.

Inventory control. The control of stock-in-trade by means of accounting controls, such as perpetual inventory records, and by means of physical control, such as proper methods of buying, storing, issuing and periodic or continuous counting of inventories on hand.

Investigation. As an accounting term, a special examination conducted for a particular purpose. Depending on the purpose, it may be more or less extensive in character than the regular shareholders' or proprietors' annual audit. Examples are an examination of operating results over a term of years for a prospective purchaser or in connection with an issue of stocks or bonds; an examination of books, vouchers, etc., in connection with fraud; an examination on behalf of a bank, finance company, or individual who is proposing to finance a business.

Investment. 1. An expenditure to acquire property which yields, or is expected to yield, revenue or service; the property so acquired. 2. See **Security 1.**

Invoice. *n.* A document prepared by the seller setting out the details of goods sold or services rendered to the purchaser including quantity, price, terms of payment, etc.

I.O.U. (*colloq.*) An informal document acknowledging a debt, setting out the amount of the debt and signed by the debtor.

Issued capital. The number or ascribed value of shares of capital stock of a limited company that have been subscribed, allotted, and entered on the share register, whether or not fully paid up. (Compare **Unissued capital.**)

Item depreciation. See **Depreciation unit.**

J

Job cost system.
Job order costing. A system of cost accounting in which costs are accumu-

lated for each unit or group of units produced. (Compare **Process cost system, process costing.**)

Joint account. 1. An account or statement of a **joint venture.** 2. A bank account which may be drawn upon individually by two or more persons.

Joint products. Differing goods produced together in the course of the processing operations, the products being in such relationship that none can be designated as the major product. (Compare **By-product.**)

Joint venture. A specific commercial undertaking entered into jointly by two or more parties or companies who agree to contribute the necessary capital and who share in profits or losses of the project in agreed proportions. The association terminates either upon completion of the undertaking or at a specific time. (Compare **Partnership.**)

Journal. 1. Any book of original entry, including the specialized journals such as the sales journal and cash journal, in addition to the general journal. 2. See **General journal.**

Journal entry. An entry in a general journal.

Journal voucher. A document supporting an entry in a general journal.

Junior security. A bond or mortgage the collateral for which has been pledged as security for other indebtedness and which is subject to these prior claims.

K

Kiting. The act of depositing in one bank account a cheque drawn on another bank account and recording only the deposit in the business' books on the day of the transfer. This has the effect of covering a cash shortage on the day of the transfer by increasing the balance of the cash in bank in the account into which the cheque was deposited without a corresponding decrease in the account against which the cheque was drawn.

L

Land improvements. Expenditures incurred in the process of putting land into a usable condition; these expenditures may include clearing, grading, levelling, landscaping, paving, installing sewer, water and gas lines, etc.

Lapping. The act of fraudulently withholding receipts which are made good by depositing subsequent receipts of cash or cheques or by fictitious entries recording erroneous sales discounts, returns and allowances or bad debt write-offs.

Last in, first out ("Lifo"). A method of allocating costs of materials or

in common or preferred shares of a subsidiary company who do not hold the controlling interest. 2. In consolidated financial statements, the amount shown as applicable to subsidiary companies' shares that are not owned by the parent company or by a consolidated subsidiary company.

Minutes. A record of the important matters discussed and decisions reached at a meeting.

Mix. *n.* The proportion of various items included in a group.

Mortgage. *n.* The written instrument of transfer of property or of a lien on property given by the borrower (mortgagor) to the lender (mortgagee) for the purpose of securing the payment of a debt.

Mortgage bond. A bond (See **Bond** 1.) secured by a mortgage.

N

Natural business year. A fiscal year ending on a date that is especially appropriate for the year end of a business, usually in a season of minimal business activity, when inventories and perhaps receivables may be expected to be relatively low. The results of operations on the natural year basis represent a matching of the costs and revenues of the same annual cycle for the business. (Compare **Fiscal period.**)

Negative confirmation. See **Confirmation** 2.

Negative goodwill. A term sometimes used in accountants' working papers to designate the excess of the book value of the net assets of a subsidiary company over the price paid by the controlling company on acquisition of the shares in the subsidiary. The term is not used in published statements, since descriptive designations are more suitable, e.g. "Excess of book value of shares in subsidiaries over their cost" or "Excess of underlying assets over the cost of investment in subsidiary companies".

Net. Not subject to any deduction, or after all applicable deductions have been made. Examples of its use are net profit, i.e. profit after deduction of all related costs; net price, i.e. the price subject to no further discounts; net sales, i.e. sales less returned sales, etc.

Net assets. The excess of the book value of the assets of a business over its liabilities to outsiders. See **Capital** 2.

Net current assets. See **Working capital.**

Net worth. The book value of the owners' equity in a business. See **Capital** 2, **Net assets.**

No par value stock. Shares of capital stock which have no specified nominal or par value.

Nominal account. An account for revenue, income, expense, or loss. (Compare **Real account.**)

Nominal rate. The ratio of income realized to the par or face value or, in the case of no par value shares, the stated value of an investment. (Compare **Effective rate.**)

Nonledger assets. Assets, such as accruals, that are not carried on the books, especially in the case of insurance companies.

Note payable. A promissory note in the hands of the debtor. Generally used in the plural to refer to both drafts and notes payable. See **Bill payable.**

Note receivable. A promissory note in the hands of the creditor. Generally used in the plural to refer to both drafts and notes receivable. See **Bill receivable.**

O

Obsolescence. The condition of becoming out of date, obsolete, or useless as a result of new discoveries, improvements, or changes in consumer demand. See **Depreciation.**

Off-line. (*machine accounting*) Relating to the operation of machines not under the direct control of the control processing unit of a mechanical or electronic data processing system. (Compare **On-line.**)

Offset. *v.* To reduce by applying opposites against each other, e.g. an account payable offset against an account receivable from the same person.

On account. 1. In partial payment. 2. On credit terms, rather than for cash.

Oncost. See **Factory overhead, Factory service.**

On-line. (*machine accounting*) Relating to the operation of machines under the direct control of the central processing unit of a mechanical or electronic data processing system. (Compare **Off-line.**)

Open account. 1. Any account which still has a balance. 2. A term of credit indicating an unsecured amount owing or receivable.

Opening entry. The first entry or one of a series of entries in the books, setting up assets, liabilities, and capital, e.g. on the formation of a new business or on establishing a new branch.

Operating. Having to do with the main or inherent activities of a business, e.g. operating revenue, operating expense, as distinguished from extraneous matters, e.g. income from temporary investments of a manufacturing concern.

Operating budget. See **Budget 2.**

Operating company. A company actively engaged in business with outsiders.

Operating cycle. The time period between the acquisition of raw materials or merchandise and the recovery of cash from the sale of the goods.

Operating ratio. 1. The percentage of total operating costs (cost of goods sold plus operating expenses) to total operating revenue such as net sales. 2. In the plural ("operating ratios"), the ratios of the various items in a profit and loss statement to net sales.

Operating statement. See **Statement, Operating.**

Opinion. 1. A judgment formed; a belief. 2. (*auditing*) The formal statement by an auditor setting out his conclusion as to the propriety of financial statements. See **Auditor's report, Audit report.**

Opportunity cost. The expected change in cost resulting from the use of an alternative asset, process, product or standard.

Option. The right of executing or relinquishing a commercial transaction within a specified period on agreed terms.

Ordinary creditor. 1. (*legal*) A creditor who, by statute, is entitled to satisfaction of his proven claim against the estate of a bankrupt, only after the claims of all other classes of creditors have been satisfied. 2. (*colloq.*) An unsecured creditor.

Organization expense. A cost incurred in the formation or incorporation of a company e.g. legal and accounting fees, registration fees, etc.

Original cost. See **Historic cost.**

Original entry. The first record of the effects of a transaction or adjustment, made in a book of original entry preparatory to the posting of the indicated debits and credits to the designated ledger accounts.

Outlay. See **Expenditure.**

Output. 1. The quantity of goods or services produced. 2. (*machine accounting*) The form (punched cards, tapes, etc.) and results of the operation of a mechanical or electronic data processing system.

Outstanding. 1. Uncollected (accounts or bills receivable). 2. Unpaid (liabilities). 3. Uncleared (cheques). 4. Unredeemed (capital stock.) 5. Unfilled (orders).

Overabsorb. To charge estimated overhead to production in excess of actual overhead. (Compare **Underabsorb.**)

Overdraft. The excess of withdrawals over the amount provided in an account such as a bank account or an appropriation account.

Overhead. Expenses which are incurred in the production of a commodity or the rendering of a service, but which cannot conveniently be measured by unit of production or service. These expenses are sometimes classified as (1) manufacturing overhead, (2) selling and distributive overhead, and (3) administrative and general overhead.

Over-the-counter. *adj.* (*security and commodity brokerage*) Relating to transactions in securities or commodities not listed on an established exchange.

P

Paid-in surplus. See **Contributed surplus.**

Paid-up capital. That part of the subscribed capital for which settlement has been received.

Paper. (*colloq.*)Bills of exchange or other negotiable evidence of indebtedness.

Paper profit. (*colloq.*) An unrealized profit, e.g. appreciation in market value of securities held, or unrealized profit arising from a change in the exchange rate where a head office has supplied goods to a foreign branch but such goods are still unsold.

Parent company. A company which controls one or more other companies through ownership of a majority of voting shares.

Participating feature. A characteristic sometimes attaching to preferred stock which provides the right to share with common stock in the distribution of profits, in addition to a fixed rate of annual dividends, and in the distribution on liquidation of the company.

Partnership. (*legal*) The relation which exists between persons carrying on a business in common with a view of profit. This does not apply, however, to the relation which exists between members of an incorporated company or association. (Compare **Joint venture.**)

Par value. The nominal or face value of a security. In connection with capital stock, that amount of authorized capital which is assigned to any particular class of stock, or to any share or shares within that class. In connection with bonds, that amount which is by the terms of issue stated to be the par value.

Passed dividend. A situation resulting from the failure to declare a dividend which would normally be paid in accordance with a company's established dividend policy; in relation to cumulative preference shares, usually described as a dividend in arrears.

Patronage dividend. See Dividend 4.

Payment. A disbursement or transfer of goods or services accepted as the equivalent of money to discharge an obligation or as a gift or loan.

Payroll. 1. The book, sheet, or other document on which are listed the names of employees and the amounts payable to them as salaries or wages at a given time, with particulars as to rate of pay, deductions, etc. 2. The total amount payable to employees at a given time or for a given period.

Pension fund. The pool of cash, investments, and other assets set aside for the payment of pensions as they fall due.

Performance budget. (*government accounting*) A budget classifying expenditures by functions or activities, rather than by objects of expenditure.

Period costs. Costs charged as expense in the period in which they are incurred and not included in the inventory valuation. (Compare **Product costs.**)

Permanent asset. A term sometimes used for a capital or fixed asset, indicating the intention to retain the asset for use throughout its working life.

Permanent file. (*auditing*) The file of working papers containing information required for reference in successive audits of a particular concern, as distinguished from working papers applicable to any one year. The permanent file may contain extracts from the instrument of incorporation and from the bylaws and minutes, information as to share capital, bond issues and long-term contracts, progressive schedules of fixed assets and depreciation, etc.

Perpetual inventory. A continuous record of the flow of merchandise and/or materials and of the stock on hand. The record may be in amounts (at cost or selling prices) or in quantities or in both amounts and quantities.

Person. (*legal*) A human being or body corporate or corporation having rights and duties before the law.

Personal account. 1. An account with a debtor or a creditor. 2. A proprietor's or partner's drawing or current account.

Personal corporation. (*income tax*) A particular type of limited company as defined by the taxing statute.

Petty cash. Cash kept on hand or in a special bank account for the purpose of meeting small payments.

Physical inventory. An inventory determined by actual count, weight, or measurement, as distinguished from a perpetual inventory or an estimated inventory.

Physical life. The period of time in which a tangible asset is in existence.

Plant. This term, as applied to business assets, has no precise meaning but is used in the following senses: (1) A collective term for the machinery, tools and equipment of a manufacturing or other industrial organization. (2) Land and buildings. (3) Buildings. (4) All of the tangible fixed property including land, buildings, equipment, etc.

Pledge. *n.* 1. A promise, binding through either moral or legal obligation. 2. A promise to contribute to a charitable or non-profit organization. (Compare **Subscription** 2.) 3. Collateral.

Pledge. *v.* 1. To give a pledge. 2. See **Hypothecate.**

Pooling of interests. A business combination where the ownership equities of the constituent businesses remain substantially unchanged.

Positive confirmation. See **Confirmation** 2.

Post. *v.* To transfer an amount to a book such as a ledger from a book of original entry or from a document.

Post-balance sheet events. Events occurring between the date of financial statements and the date of the audit report on such statements.

Posting. *n.* The entry or amount posted in an account.

Posting medium. Any book, file, or document from which entries are posted to the ledger, e.g. a journal, cash book, voucher register, invoice, duplicate receipt, etc.

Postulate. 1. See **Accounting principle** 1. 2. (*pl.*) The basic assumptions on which accounting principles are founded.

Practice. 1. A professional partnership's or individual's clientele *"in toto"*, or his business. 2. (*accounting*) A general term referring to methods or procedures used in accounting.

Practise. To carry on business as a professional individual.

Pre-audit. An examination performed before proceeding with a commitment, expenditure, payment, or other specified transaction, e.g. examination of contracts, purchase orders, appropriations, by-law requirements, and invoices, before payment of accounts.

Preferred creditor. (*legal*) A creditor who, by statute, is entitled to full satisfaction of his proven claim against the estate of a bankrupt before other unsecured creditors receive anything.

Preference shares.
Preferred shares.
Preferred stock. A class of share capital with special rights or restrictions as compared with other classes of stock of the same company. The preference will generally attach to the distribution of dividends at a stipulated rate, with or without priority for return of capital on winding up, but the nature of the preferences can vary widely according to the terms of issue. Such shares normally have no voting rights to elect the company's directors.

Preliminary expense. 1. Organization expense. 2. More broadly, a general term for organization, development, and other pre-production expenses.

Premium. 1. The amount by which the selling price of a security exceeds the par value. 2. The consideration payable for the purchase of insurance protection or for an annuity contract.

Prepaid expense. 1. A short term expense prepayment; an expenditure, other than a capital expenditure, which is expected to yield its benefits in the near future and meanwhile is carried forward to be assigned to expense in the near future. (Compare **Deferred charge** 1.) 2. Balance of amounts paid for services not yet received from the payee and which meanwhile is carried forward to be assigned to expense in future years. (Compare **Deferred charge** 2.)

Present fairly. 1. To show, exhibit or display equitably and impartially. 2. (*auditing*) As used in the auditor's report, this phrase means that the financial position and operating results as reflected by the financial statements are believed to be substantially correct and not misleading.

Present value. The discounted value of a future payment or payments; the amount which, when invested at a fixed rate of interest and compounded at regular periods, will accumulate to a specified sum at a given future date.

Price-earnings ratio. The market price per share of stock divided by the company's earnings per share.

Price leader. See **Loss leader.**

Price leadership. The position held by a business with a sufficiently large share of a market that changes in the selling price of its products will result in similar price changes by its competitors.

Price maintenance. The action of a manufacturer, wholesaler or jobber who induces his retailers to sell his products to the public at not less than a specified price.

Price variance. The difference between the standard cost of direct material and labour and the actual cost resulting from changes in price.

Prime cost. The direct cost of production, i.e. **direct labour** and **direct material.**

Principal. 1. The capital amount of an investment or loan. 2. The capital moneys, funds, investments and other properties of estates (that is, the estate "corpus"), endowments, etc., as distinguished from income. 3. (*legal*) An individual or company employing another individual or company (the agent) to make contracts on its behalf with third individuals or companies.

Principle. See **Accounting principle.**

Private company. 1. A limited company classified as a private company by virtue of the provisions of the Act under which it was incorporated and the provisions of its letters patent, supplementary letters patent or memorandum of association. 2. (*colloq.*) A limited company whose shares are not listed on a recognized stock exchange or otherwise available to the public investor.

Private ledger. A ledger in which selected confidential accounts are kept, these accounts usually being represented in the general ledger by a controlling account, although the general ledger itself is frequently regarded as a private ledger and may be so called.

Pro forma. *adj.* A term applied to a document drawn up after giving effect to stated assumptions or contractual commitments which have not yet been completed.

Procedural review. (*auditing*) A review of internal controls and other procedures of an organization for the purpose of assessing their efficiency and reliability.

Procedure. A method or course of action.

Process cost system.
Process costing. A system of cost accounting in which costs are accumulated in respect of each department or phase of production in such a manner that the cost (and thus, the unit cost) of each such department or phase of production may be ascertained. (Compare **Job cost system, Job order costing.**)

Product. 1. A commodity produced by the manufacturing processes, or a service rendered by a business. 2. (*math.*) The result of multiplying two or more figures together.

Product costs. Costs associated with the product, and thus included in determining costs of goods sold and inventory valuations. (Compare **Period costs.**)

Production or **service-output method.** See **Depreciation method.**

Productive wages. See **Direct labour.**

Profession. A society whose members (i) avow knowledge of some department of learning, which knowledge is applied to the affairs of others, (ii) recognize their responsibility to the public and their clients, and (iii) subscribe to a code of ethical behaviour.

Profit. *n.* 1. The excess of revenues over expenses for a period, usually referred to as "*net* profit". 2. The excess of the proceeds of the sale of an asset over its cost or unamortized cost. 3. (*economics*) An increase in value measured in terms of constant purchasing power.

Profit and loss account. 1. The ledger account to which the balances of the revenue, income, expense, and loss accounts at the end of an accounting period are transferred, to show the net differences as the profit or loss for the period. This net difference is then transferred to earned surplus account or some other appropriate proprietorship account. 2. The statement of profit and loss.

Profit and loss statement.
Profit and loss, Statement of. See **Statement of profit and loss.**

Programme. *n.* 1. A definite plan to be followed in carrying out a procedure. 2. (*auditing*) See **Audit programme.**

Programme. *v.* (*machine accounting*) To establish a sequence of instructions which cause or enable a mechanical or electronic data processing system to carry out a specific operation.

Promissory note. An unconditional promise in writing made by one person to another, signed by the maker, promising to pay on demand or at a fixed or determinable future time, a sum certain in money to or to the order of a specified person or to bearer.

Proof of loss. (*insurance*) A statement setting out in detail the claim of an assured with respect to a loss claimed to be recoverable by him under the terms of a contract of insurance.

Proposal. 1. A scheme or plan for action. 2. A scheme for extension of time and/or reduction of debt put forward to creditors by a debtor under the terms of the *Bankruptcy Act* or the *Companies' Creditors Arrangement Act.* When accepted by a stipulated portion of the creditors and approved by the court, its terms are binding upon all parties to the proposal.

Proprietorship. 1. The total equity of the owners of a business; the capital and surplus as revealed by the balance sheet at any time. 2. See **Sole proprietorship.**

Prospectus. The formal document which a company is usually required to issue when inviting the public to subscribe to its share capital or bonds.

Provision. 1. An estimated expense. 2. (*obs.*) An allowance for a diminution in value of an asset or an estimated or accrued liability.

Public accountant. 1. A person who alone or in partnership with others for reward engages in public practice involving: (i) the performance of services which include causing to be prepared, signed, delivered or issued any financial, accounting or related statement, or (ii) the issuing of any written opinion, report or certificate concerning such statement, if by reason of the signature, stationery or wording employed or otherwise it is indicated that such individual or partnership acts in relation to the said statement, opinion, report or certificate as an independent accountant or auditor, or as an individual having or purporting to have expert knowledge in accounting or auditing matters. Despite the generality of the foregoing, "Public Accountant" usually does not include a person who acts merely as bookkeeper, cost accountant, or on the installation of bookkeeping, business or cost systems, nor does it include a person who performs accounting or auditing functions in respect of: any public authority or any commission, committee or emanation thereof, including a Crown company, any bank, loan or trust company, and transportation company incorporated by Act of the Parliament of Canada; or any other publicly-owned or publicly-controlled public utility organization. 2. A meaning given by a particular statute.

Public accounting. 1. The professional practice of accounting and related services offered to the public for a fee, generally including auditing, the services of tax consultation, consultation as to accounting systems and procedures, investigation and any other similar services. 2. A meaning given by a particular statute.

Public company. 1. A limited company which is not a private company as provided by the Act under which the company was incorporated. 2. (*colloq.*) A limited company whose shares are available to the public investor.

Purchase book.

Purchase journal. A book of original entry in which purchases on credit terms are recorded.

Purchase order. A form used to place an order for goods or services with a supplier.

Q

Qualification. An expansion in an auditor's report setting forth a limitation or modification of his opinion as to the fairness of the financial statements in accordance with generally accepted accounting principles applied on a basis consistent with that of the preceding year.

Qualified report. An auditor's report that includes a qualification.

Qualifying share. A share in a limited company required to be held by a director of the company.

Quantity discount. A reduction in the selling price of goods or services granted by a vendor in consideration of the large number of units purchased in an individual transaction. (Compare **Volume discount.**)

Quick assets. 1. Cash on hand or at bank, marketable securities held temporarily, accounts receivable within the normal term of credit, short term trade bills receivable. 2. The total thereof.

R

Rate of exchange. The price, in one country's currency, at which the currency of another country may be bought or sold.

Rating. *n.* An indication of the relative degree of desirability or competence by reference to recognized standards, e.g. A-1 credit rating is indicative of a good credit risk.

Ratio analysis. The study of various ratios in the analysis of financial statements to evaluate financial condition, operations, and related factors.

Raw material. A commodity acquired for the purpose of being consumed or changed in form in the manufacturing process. (Compare **Direct material.**)

Real account. An account for any asset or liability. (Compare **Nominal account.**)

Real estate. Land and improvements, including buildings, standing timber, orchard trees, etc.

Realization account. An account sometimes used in the liquidation of an estate or business, and in which the amounts realized on sale of the assets are set off against the book values of the assets, thus showing the profit or loss on realization.

Realization and liquidation, Statement of. See **Statement of realization and liquidation.**

Realized income.
Realized profit. The income or profit that results from a completed transaction which will produce an ascertainable amount of cash.

Rebate. A price allowance or refund.

Recapitalization. A voluntary adjustment in the share capital structure of a limited company. It may involve changes in both the nature and amount of various classes of shares, capitalization of contributed and earned surplus, elimination of deficit, elimination of preferred dividend arrears, etc. (Compare **Refinancing, Reorganization.**)

Receipt. 1. The act of receiving money or merchandise. 2. The amount of money received. 3. A signed acknowledgement of the receipt of money or merchandise.

Receipts and disbursements, Statement of. See **Statement of receipts and disbursements.**

Reconciliation.
Reconciliation statement. 1. Any statement accounting for the differences between two related records. Generally applied to the statement drawn up to account for the difference between a bank balance as reflected in the books of a bank and the balance of the same account as reflected in the books of the bank's customer. 2. A statement accounting for differences or changes during a period, e.g. a "reconciliation of earned surplus".

Record date. The date selected by the board of directors of a limited company for determination of the shareholders to whom a dividend is to be paid.

Redeemable preferred stock. Preferred shares callable for redemption at the option of the company in accordance with conditions determined by charter or by-law.

Redemption fund. A name sometimes given to a sinking fund established for the retirement of a debt.

Redemption price.
Redemption value. The price payable on redemption of securities.

Reducing balance method.
Reducing instalment method. See **Depreciation method—Diminishing balance.**

Refinancing. A voluntary adjustment in the financial structure of a business; may involve changes in the nature and amount of share capital and/or of funded debt. (Compare **Recapitalization, Reorganization.**)

Refunding. The exchange of a currently maturing liability for one which matures at some more distant date in the future. Refunding can be effected by arrangement with the present creditor or by borrowing from a third party to obtain funds to discharge the obligation to the present creditor.

Registrar. An employee or agent of a limited company responsible for the maintenance of its shareholders' and bondholders' records. (Compare **Transfer agent.**)

Reinsurance. A contract between insurers whereby one assumes part of the risk on an insurance contract issued by the other.

Related company. See **Affiliated company, Associated corporation.**

Renegotiation. A process of revision of government contracts, often involving adjustment of the contract price after completion of the work. The aim is to leave the final determination of prices on such contracts until the profit can be ascertained.

Renewal (of plant). Replacement of parts or other restoration designed to extend the useful life of the asset beyond the normal life. Replacement of the whole asset is not usually called a renewal. Improvements which alter the original form of the asset are preferably referred to as improvements or betterments rather than as renewals. Where renewals are not material in cost, they are generally classified as repairs.

Renewal accounting. An accounting procedure in which the cost of a fixed asset is charged to expense when replacement occurs, such charge being the cost of the replacement rather than the cost of the original asset. (Compare **Depreciation accounting, Retirement accounting.**)

Rent roll. A record of rents receivable kept by an owner of property or his agent.

Reorganization. A major change in the financial structure, management or policies of a business. (Compare **Recapitalization, Refinancing.**)

Repair. Replacement of parts or other restoration of units of plant, designed to restore normal working efficiency. (Compare **Improvement, Maintenance.**)

Replacement. 1. Substitution of one asset for another, usually the substitution of a new unit of plant for an old unit. 2. The installation of a new part in place of an old part, in this sense being the same as either **renewal** or **repair.**

Replacement accounting. 1. See **Renewal accounting.** 2. A method of accounting for assets in which the replacement cost of some or all assets is used as the basis for presenting the assets in financial statements.

Replacement cost.
Replacement value. The current cost of replacing an asset with another which will render similar services.

Report form (of statement). A vertical arrangement of the items in a financial statement. See **Balance sheet, Form of.** (Compare **Account form.**)

Reproduction cost. The current cost of reproducing a specified property in identical form.

Requisition. A form of request, usually on official stationery, for specified articles, services, or cash to be supplied by one department to another.

Reservation. See **Qualification.**

Reserve. 1. An amount appropriated from net profits or other surplus, at the discretion of management or pursuant to the requirements of a statute, the instrument of incorporation or by-laws of a company or a trust indenture or other agreement, for a specific or general purpose such as general contingencies, possible future declines in inventory values, future plant extensions, and redemption of stocks and bonds. The reserve indicates that an undivided or unidentified portion of the net assets, in a stated amount, is being held or retained for general or specific purposes. 2. (*obs.*) The term was inappropriately used in the past to describe: (a) Allowance for doubtful accounts and accumulated allowance for depreciation. (b) A liability, the amount of which can only be estimated. (c) A receipt for services or goods to be supplied in the future. (d) A refundable deposit or charge. (e) A charge, in the statement of profit and loss, with respect to such expenses as doubtful accounts, depreciation, taxes, etc.

Reserve fund. A pool of designated assets, usually cash and investment securities, earmarked for the purpose of a specified reserve, e.g. sinking fund for bond redemption.

Residual value. 1. The balance of the original cost of an asset less any portion thereof amortized or treated as an expense or loss. 2. The value remaining to an asset which has served its economically useful life; the scrap value.

Resources. The total assets available to a concern to meet its liabilities. Sometimes includes non-ledger assets, such as uncalled portions of share subscriptions.

Responsibility costing. A system of cost accounting in which costs are accumulated according to the expenditures incurred in each area of managerial responsibility.

Rest account. The general reserve account of a bank.

Retail method. A method of inventory valuation whereby purchases of merchandise are recorded at cost and at selling prices. By comparing the aggregate cost of the opening inventory and purchases, for any period, with the corresponding selling value, a ratio of cost to selling price is determined. The estimated cost of merchandise on hand can be calculated at any time by applying this ratio to inventory at selling prices determined by subtracting sales for the period from total goods available for sale at selling prices. This same ratio is used in converting book or physical inventory valued at selling prices to estimated cost.

Retained earnings. See **Earned surplus.**

Retirement accounting. An accounting procedure in which no charge to expense is made for a fixed asset until it is removed from service, the whole original cost being charged against operations in the year in which the asset is retired. (Compare **Depreciation accounting, Renewal accounting.**)

Return. *n.* 1. A statement of information required by governmental bodies from individuals and companies. 2. Amount earned on an investment. 3. Relation of net profit to gross sales.

Returns. In commercial usage, items of merchandise returned by a purchaser to the vendor, e.g. sales returns, in the vendor's books; purchase returns, in the purchaser's books.

Revaluation reserve.
Revaluation surplus. (*obs.*) A term formerly used to describe the credit balance resulting from the adjustment of the recorded value of long-term assets to a higher value as established by an appraisal in the case of fixed assets and by prevailing market prices in the case of investments. In effect, this is a valuation account representing unrealized increases in value and should, therefore, not be designated as either a "reserve" or "surplus". More suitable terminology would be "Excess of appraisal value of fixed assets (or market value of long-term investments) over cost".

Revenue. 1. The gross proceeds of the sale of goods and services (generally after deducting returns, allowances and discounts), gains from the sale or exchange of assets (other than stock-in-trade), interest and dividends earned on investments and other realized increases in owners' equity in a business except those arising as a result of capital contributions and adjustments. (Compare **Income.**) 2. (*government accounting*) The gross amounts received and receivable from taxes, licences, duties and other sources.

Revenue and expenditure, Statement of. See **Statement of revenue and expenditure.**

Revenue and expense, Statement of. See **Statement of profit and loss.**

Revenue expenditure. Expense.

Revenue receipts. A term used for **revenue** by some governmental units reporting on a cash basis.

Reversing entry. 1. In particular, the plural (reversing entries) refers to a group of entries made at the beginning of an accounting period to bring into account for the period any deferred or accrued amounts adjusted at the end of the preceding period. 2. (*colloq.*) A correcting entry.

Review. *v.* (*auditing*) To examine or re-examine critically.

Revolving fund. A fund provided for a particular purpose which is constantly or periodically replenished either from operations or by transfers from other funds, e.g. a working capital fund provided to finance branch or departmental operations; an imprest petty cash fund.

Right. See **Share right.**

Round sum. (*colloq.*) A figure which has been expressed in even tens, hundreds, thousands, etc., so that only significant digits are included.

Royalty. An agreed amount payable to the owner of certain rights or commodities for the privilege of using or exploiting them. The royalty is normally based on the income derived from the use of the property in question, as in the case of a royalty to the copyright owner of a book, a royalty to the owner of a patent, or a royalty to the government or other owner for the right to mine or conduct logging operations on certain property.

S

Sales. In accounting reports, the designation of the total amount of proceeds of disposition of stock-in-trade, and sometimes of services, net of returns and allowances. The terms "gross sales" and "net sales" are sometimes used to distinguish the sales aggregate before and after deduction of returns and allowances.

Salvage value. The realizable value of assets which are no longer usable or salable on normal terms, especially as a result of damage by fire or other accident. The salvage value is that portion which can be reconditioned for future use the remainder being disposed of for the scrap value of its material content. (Compare **Scrap value.**)

Saw-off. (*colloq.*) A compromise.

Scan. (*auditing*) To review data in order to locate significant items which may require further study. (Compare **Scrutinize.**)

Schedule. 1. A tabulated list of items. 2. A supplementary statement giving details of an item or items on a main statement.

Scrap value. The realizable value of metal or other material content of an asset, exclusive of components which may be removed for use, remaining upon cessation of the asset's functional usefulness. (Compare **Salvage value.**)

Scrutinize. (*auditing*) To review data searchingly in order to locate significant items which may require further study. (Compare **Scan.**)

Secret reserve. An amount by which the owners' equity in a business has been understated on the business' records as a result of an undervaluation or omission of assets or an overstatement of liabilities. This term does not represent a specific account bearing that name or disclosed in financial statements but rather a condition which exists.

Secured creditor. (*legal*) One to whom a secured liability is owed. See **Secured liability.**

Secured liability. A debt in support of which the debtor has pledged to the creditor certain assets or guarantees.

Security. 1. A bond or share or other document evidencing debt or ownership. 2. Collateral.

Self-balancing ledger. A ledger in which the total of the accounts with debit balances should equal the total of the accounts with credit balances.

Self insurance. The assumption by an individual or a company of a risk of loss which otherwise might have been the subject of an insurance contract.

Sellers' market. A condition within an industry or geographic area where the demand for a product or service exceeds the supply; hence trading conditions favour the seller. (Compare **Buyers' market.**)

Selling expense. The classification for financial statement purposes of those expenses of an organization relating to the selling or marketing of the organization's goods or services; as opposed to those expenses incurred for other specialized functions such as administration, financial, and manufacturing.

Semi variable cost.
Semi variable expense. A cost which varies with production or activity but not in direct proportion to the volume. The term refers to indirect expenses. (Compare **Fixed cost, Fixed expense, Variable cost, Variable expense.**)

Serial bonds. Bonds of an issue which provides for annual or other periodical redemption of instalments of principal, each instalment consisting of one or several bonds.

Service-output method. See **Depreciation method.**

Setup time. The length of time required to change machines or methods of production due to a change in product.

Share. One of the equal parts into which each class of the capital stock of a limited company is divided, representing a proportionate interest in the total equity of all shares of the same class.

Share capital. Capital of a limited company represented by shares of capital stock as distinct from surplus and capital represented by bonded or other indebtedness. (Compare **Capital stock.**)

Share ledger.
Share register. The book or other register required to be kept by a limited company to show particulars as to shares held by each shareholder.

Shareholder. The person in whose name one or more shares of a limited company are registered in the company's share register.

Shareholders' equity. The interest of the shareholders in the assets of a limited company. The term is often applied to the total of the share capital and surplus items in the balance sheet.

Share right. A privilege granted by a limited company to a shareholder which entitles him to purchase his proportionate share of a new issue of capital stock, usually at a fixed price and within a stated period of time. A certificate, which is transferable, is usually issued to indicate the number of shares which the holder is entitled to purchase. (Compare **Stock purchase warrant.**)

Share warrant. A certificate for fully paid shares indicating the ownership represented in a limited company; a bearer share certificate. Dividend coupons are usually attached. Share warrants are now rarely issued.

Short position. (*security or commodity brokerage*) A condition where the broker is entitled to receive securities or commodities; a person required to deliver securities or commodities to a broker is said to be "short" those securities or commodities in the broker's accounts. (Compare **Long position.**)

Short sale. Usually a sale of a security or commodity not owned by the vendor, in anticipation of a fall in the market price when a profit may be realized by a purchase which will enable the vendor to deliver the required security or commodity.

Short-term liability. See **Current liability.**

Short-term rate. (*insurance*) A rate, higher than the normal rate, which is applied when an insurance contract (other than life insurance) is cancelled prior to its expiry date or issued for a shorter-than-normal period at the request of the insured.

Single entry bookkeeping. A form of bookkeeping in which only cash books and/or personal accounts are maintained. (Compare **Double entry bookkeeping.**)

Single proprietorship. See **Sole proprietorship.**

Single step income statement. That form of income statement in which no successive gradations of income or loss are shown but, instead, all items of revenue or gain are grouped and extended in one total, as are all items of expense or loss, the latter being deducted from the former to arrive at a single figure of net income or net loss for the period.

Sinking fund. A pool of cash and investments, usually built up systematically, earmarked to provide resources for the redemption of debt or capital stock.

Sinking fund method. See **Depreciation method.**

Sinking fund reserve. A portion of surplus appropriated for retention for the purposes of a sinking fund.

Small tools. Inexpensive equipment which will be used up in a relatively short time in the course of operations. Such items are usually charged to expense upon acquisition, although they may be valued at year end on an inventory basis.

Social accounting. The preparation and interpretation of overall economic statistics in financial statement form. Social accounting, like business accounting, is concerned with the double entry recording of transaction, the presentation of financial data in statement form, and the measurement of income, but embraces larger sectors of society, such as consumers, governments, foreigners, or business enterprises as a whole. It is directed toward the data of national income, gross national product, gross national expenditure, production, consumption, investment, and saving. The main types of statements involved are: 1. The national income and product "account". 2. The balance of international payments statement. 3. Flow of funds statements for various sectors of the economy, e.g. manufacturing, utilities, persons, governments, etc. 4. Input-output tables, to show the economic relationship as to receipts and expenditures of the various sectors, identified for example as various types of businesses, governments, and households.

Sole proprietorship. An unincorporated business wholly owned by one person.

Source and application of funds, Statement of.
Source and disposition of funds, Statement of. See **Statement of source and application of funds.**

Special audit. 1. An examination limited in scope; an investigation. 2. An audit other than a continuously recurring annual audit.

Specific identification. A method of cost determination by which the cost for each individual item in an inventory is ascertained separately.

Spot check. 1. (*colloq.*) (*auditing*) An arbitrary selection in a test audit. 2. (*colloq.*) (*auditing*) A surprise count (usually of cash, securities or inventories).

Staff auditor. An internal auditor.

Standard. 1. A basis for comparison. As used in the term "standard costs", the basis may indicate normal, anticipated, or ideal performance, or it may represent merely a fixed base by means of which variation in performance may be measured. 2. An accepted or established rule or model.

Standard cost. A predetermined or estimated cost of any product or operation, comprising the elements of cost, namely labour, materials, and overhead; a selected target figure for such cost, used as a basis of comparison.

Standard cost system.
Standard costing. Accounting procedures in which actual costs of production are compared with predetermined standards, generally by means of analysis of the variations as price, time, quantity, and efficiency variances.

Standing order. 1. A work order issued as authority for the production of articles for stock, as opportunity arises, and probably limited by a stated maximum. 2. An order issued as authority for the purchase of goods or services to be made as required or up to a stated total amount.

Stated value. 1. See **Book value** 1. 2. The amount at which the capital stock of a limited company is carried in the accounts; in the case of par value shares, the par value, and in the case of no par value shares, the amount (or amounts) determined by a resolution (or resolutions) of the board of directors.

Statement. 1. A copy of one or more personal accounts. 2. Any presentation of financial data in a more or less formal arrangement. See **Financial statement.**

Statement, Cash. See **Statement of receipts and disbursements.**

Statement, Cash flow. A statement, for a stated period, showing the net effect of various kinds of business transactions on the cash position. It is similar to the statement of source and application of funds except that the cash flow statement also takes into account changes, other than cash, in current assets and liabilities. (Compare **Statement of receipts and disbursements.**)

Statement, Common-size. A statement in which the various items are expressed as a percent of a specific item included in the statement; in the case of the balance sheet, the total assets and the total equities respectively, and in the case of the statement of profit and loss, the net sales.

Statement, Manufacturing. A statement showing the particulars of the cost of making or all of the products of a business.

Statement of account. See **Statement** 1.

Statement of affairs. 1. A statement of assets and liabilities drawn up to indicate the amounts which may be expected to be realized if the debtor's property is sold, and the manner in which the proceeds of such sale will be distributable, having regard to the interests of preferred, secured, and unsecured creditors. 2. (*obs.*) A statement of financial position, similar to a balance sheet, but prepared otherwise than from double entry bookkeeping records.

Statement of charge and discharge. An official statement as to (a) capital or principal, and (b) income, in which an executor or administrator may be required to account to the court for receipts and dispositions of cash and/or other assets in a deceased person's estate or in a trust.

Statement of income. See **Statement of profit and loss.**

Statement of profit and loss. A statement of a business summarizing the revenues, incomes, expenses and losses for a stated period. The statement may also be appropriately described as the "income statement" or "statement of revenue and expenses". (Compare **Statement of revenue and expenditure.**)

Statement of realization and liquidation. A statement drawn up by a trustee or liquidator to account for the winding up of a business, showing the amounts realized on disposition of the assets and the amounts disbursed to liquidate the liabilities.

Statement of receipts and disbursements. A statement, for a stated period, showing the opening and closing balances of cash on hand and in bank and summarizing the cash receipts and disbursements during the period. (Compare **Statement, Cash flow.**)

Statement of revenue and expenditure. A statement summarizing the revenues and expenditure (as opposed to expenses) for a stated period. It is most often used by governmental and other non-profit organizations. (Compare **Statement of profit and loss.**)

Statement of revenue and expense. See **Statement of profit and loss.**

Statement of source and application (or disposition) of funds. A statement summarizing, for a stated period, the inward and outward movements of the working capital of a business. The difference between the funds made available and the applications will be shown as the increase or decrease in working capital during the period.

Statement, Operating. 1. A statement of profit and loss. 2. That portion of the statement of profit and loss which sets off operating expenses against operating revenue to arrive at operating profit.

Statistical sampling. A test, the extent and interpretation of which is determined by the use of statistical methods.

Statutory audit. An audit carried out in conformance with the provisions of a statute, such as a Companies Act, *The Bank Act*, a Municipal Act.

Stock. 1. See **Capital stock.** 2. See **Stock-in-trade.**

Stock dividend. A dividend payable by issue of shares of capital stock either of the same or a different class from that in respect of which the dividend is payable.

Stock-in-trade. Raw materials, goods in process and finished goods held for manufacture or for sale in the ordinary course of business.

Stock option. A right, granted by a limited company, to purchase a specified number of shares of the company's capital stock at a fixed price within a stated period of time.

Stock purchase warrant. A certificate usually attached to preferred shares or bonds of a limited company giving the owner the right to purchase a specified number of shares of the company's capital stock at a fixed price within a stated period. Warrants are sometimes marketable and sold separately. (Compare **Share right.**)

Stock split. Subdivision of a class of share capital into a greater number of shares.

Stockholder. See **Shareholder.**

Stores. 1. (*manufacturing*) Direct or indirect materials. Sometimes, but not generally, goods in process and finished goods are included as classes of stores. 2. (*wholesaling and retailing*) Finished goods and supplies. 3. (*servicing*) Supplies.

Straight line method. See Depreciation method.

"Street" form of security. See Bearer security.

Subscription. 1. A contract with a publisher providing for the delivery by the publisher of a periodical publication for a stated length of time. 2. A commitment to contribute to an enterprise or charitable or non-profit organization. (Compare **Pledge** 2.) 3. An agreement to purchase shares of a limited company.

Subsidiary company. A limited company in which a corporation (the parent or holding company) owns a majority of the shares carrying the right to elect at least a majority of the members of the board of directors. (For specific conditions in particular cases, see the definition in the appropriate statute, e.g. Companies Act.)

Subsidiary ledger. A ledger in which similar accounts, e.g. customers' accounts, are kept in detail, while the aggregate of these accounts is maintained in a control account in the general ledger.

Sum of the years' digits method. See Depreciation method.

Supplies. Materials which do not become part of the physical content of the finished product but which are consumed in the operations.

Surplus. In accounting and finance, the excess of the net assets over the total stated value of the share capital of a limited company; realized increases in owners' equity in a limited company over the capital contributed for or assigned to shares presently outstanding. Items of surplus are usually classified according to their source: contributed and earned. See **Contributed surplus** and **Earned surplus.**

Suspense account. An account to which an entry for a transaction may be posted tentatively until the correct disposition is determined, e.g. on receipt of cash from an unidentified source.

Syndicate. See Joint venture.

System of accounts. See Accounting system.

T

Tangible assets.
Tangibles. All assets except the intangible assets such as goodwill, patents, copyrights, trademarks.

Tax lien. (*government accounting*) An encumbrance placed upon a taxpayer's property as security for unpaid taxes.

Tax roll. (*government accounting*) A record of persons or companies subject to taxation, including the amount of taxes levied.

Test. *n.* The examination of a sample of items selected from a larger number, with the object of judging the general standard of accuracy or quality of the whole on the basis of the sample.

Tickler file. A record of items maintained to call attention to each item at the proper time for it to be dealt with.

Time deposit. An amount placed on deposit with a bank or trust company for a specific minimum period of time. Withdrawal is usually subject to advance notice of a specified number of days.

Trace. *v.* (*auditing*) To follow a business transaction through the various phases in the business records.

Trade acceptance. A bill of exchange given in respect of goods or services which have been supplied to the acceptor of the draft.

Trade account payable. A debt for goods or services purchased in the ordinary course of business. See also **Account payable.**

Trade account receivable. An amount claimed against a customer for goods or services sold to him in the ordinary course of business. See also **Account receivable.**

Trade discount. A deduction from the list price of goods, reducing the price to that payable by a merchant purchasing the goods for resale.

a percentage allowed off the list or catalogue price.

Trading account. 1. (*obs.*) An account sometimes used to assemble the cost of goods sold (comprising purchases and costs connected therewith, adjusted for opening and closing inventories) and to set this off against sales for the same period, to show the gross margin. 2. (*security and commodity brokerage*) An account in which is recorded frequent buy and sell transactions by a broker or his customers.

Transfer agent. An agent of a limited company responsible for the issue and cancellation of the company's bond or share certificates and the recording thereof. (Compare **Registrar.**)

Treasury stock. 1. (*U.S.*) Shares acquired by purchase by the issuing company and legally available for re-issue. In Canada, such purchase is not within the powers of limited companies (except that, in some jurisdictions, a limited company can hold fractional shares acquired as a result of a reorganization). 2. (*colloq.*) Authorized but unissued shares.

Trial balance. A list of all balances or debit and credit totals in a ledger usually showing the account numbers or names with the balances set out in the debit and credit columns. See **Balance.** *v.*

Trust fund. Property (especially cash and securities) which has been conveyed or assigned to a trustee to be dealt with by him as directed, normally by a document such as a trust deed, statute or minute.

Turnover. 1. The number of times a specified class of assets is disposed of during a given period, normally the accounting year. Thus the inventory turnover for a period is the cost of goods sold divided by the average inventory at cost; the turnover of receivables is the total credit sales for the period divided by the average amount of accounts receivable. 2. (*colloq.*) Total sales volume.

U

Unappropriated earned surplus. See **Earned surplus.**

Underabsorb. *v.* To charge to production estimated overhead which is less than actual overhead. (Compare **Overabsorb.**)

Underwriter. 1. An insurer; so called from writing his name under the contract of insurance. 2. A person who, alone or with others, and with the knowledge of the issuing company, subscribes for part or all of an issue of securities with a view to reselling them. 3. *The Companies Act* (Canada) extends the meaning to include any person to whom a commission is to be paid for subscribing or getting subscriptions for securities of the company to be offered to the public.

Underwriting commission. Commission payable to an underwriter of an issue of securities.

Unencumbered. (*government accounting*) The unexpended portion of a budget appropriation or allotment free of expenditure commitments. See **Encumbrance** 1.

Unexpended. (*government accounting*) The portion of a budget appropriation or allotment which has not been paid out, although commitments for its expenditure may have been made.

Unexpired cost. The portion of an expenditure whose benefit has not been exhausted; an asset. (Compare **Expired cost.**)

Uniform cost accounting. The general application of a set of principles and procedures of cost accounting, as for example on an industry-wide basis through the medium of a trade association or other agency.

Unincorporated business. A business organization which is not a legal entity separate from its owners or members.

Unissued capital. The portion of a limited company's authorized capital stock for which shares have not been subscribed, allotted and entered on the company's share register. (Compare **Issued capital.**)

Unit cost. The cost of a unit of product or service, found by dividing the total costs for a given period or for a given operation by the number of units produced in that period or operation.

Unit depreciation

Unit depreciation. See **Depreciation unit.**

Unpaid dividend. A dividend which has been declared, and is therefore a legal obligation but which has not been distributed. See **Dividend** 1. and 2.

Unrealized profit. The anticipated profit that will result from a transaction when the transaction is completed.

Unsecured account. An account receivable or an account payable, in support of which no collateral has been given.

Upset price. The lowest price at which a vendor is willing to sell.

Useful life. The period during which an asset is physically capable of providing a service. (Compare **Economic life.**)

V

Variable budget. A flexible budget.

Variable cost.
Variable expense. An expense that varies directly with the volume of business. (Compare **Fixed cost, Fixed expense, Semi-variable cost, Semi-variable expense.**)

Variance. (*standard costing*) The difference between actual cost and standard cost of a cost element, e.g. material price variance, material quantity variance, labour price variance, etc.

Verification. (*auditing*) The procedures for establishing the acceptability of entries, records, or statements.

Volume discount. A reduction in the selling price of goods or services granted by a vendor in consideration of the large number of units purchased in a series of transactions over a stated period. (Compare **Quantity discount.**)

Voting trust. (*Chiefly U.S.*) A group of shareholders or bondholders of a limited company who have deposited their securities with specific individuals who will, as trustees, cast the votes to which the group is entitled, in the interests of the group. Members of the group receive certificates of beneficial ownership in exchange for their actual securities.

Vouch. To verify entries or other records by examination of supporting documents.

Voucher. Any evidence of a documentary nature in support of a book entry.

Voucher register. A book of original entry for expenditure vouchers.

Voucher system. A system of recording expenditures, using a **voucher register** which combines the functions of a book of original entry for expenditures and a subsidiary record of vouchers payable.

W

Warehouse receipt. Documentary evidence issued by the warehouseman that goods are being held in storage in a public warehouse on behalf of the owner.

Warrant. *n.* 1. See **Share warrant, Stock purchase warrant.** 2. A writ allowing law officers to arrest, search, detain, seize or carry out sentence. 3. *Governor General's Warrant.* Special authority under an Order-in-Council, allowing, when Parliament is not in session, for the payment of unforeseen or emergency expenditures. Its use is severely restricted and the amounts involved are usually presented to Parliament in the succeeding estimates.

Warranty. *n.* A written statement promising remedial action on the part of the vendor if defects are found in goods sold during a stated period. (Compare **Guarantee.**)

Warranty repairs. Repairs to goods sold under warranty, the expense of the repairs being borne by the vendor or manufacturer.

Warranty repairs, Provision for. An estimated liability for future repairs to goods sold under warranty.

Wasting assets. Natural resources which are subject to exhaustion through the process of extraction or use, e.g. mineral deposits, timber limits, oil pools.

Watered stock. (*colloq.*) Share capital issued for a consideration, the fair market value of which is less than the stated value of the share.

Wear and tear. Physical deterioration of an asset through use.

Window-dressing. (*colloq.*) A generic term applied to methods of improperly enhancing the picture shown by financial statements.

Working capital. The excess of the total of the current assets over the total of the current liabilities.

Working papers. Schedules, transcripts, analyses, confirmations, notes and other memoranda prepared and accumulated by an accountant or auditor in the course of an engagement.

Work in process.

Work in progress. Partly finished goods or contracts which are in the process of manufacture or completion.

71

Work order

Work order. Written authority for the execution of specified work usually with specifications for the materials to be issued and the labour to be employed.

Write-down. *v.* To record an unrealized decrease in the value of an asset or liability.

Write-off. *n.* An amount which has been written off.

Write-off. *v.* To transfer to profit and loss or surplus all or a portion of the balance in an account previously regarded as an asset or liability.

Write up. *v.* 1. To record an unrealized increase in the value of an asset or liability. 2. To enter transactions in the books of account.

Y

Yield. 1. The amount or quantity produced. 2. See **Effective rate.**

Balancing accts

Posture side — all, Assets - Dr
all capital is cr.
all liabilities is cr

assets - liabilities = Capital   if its |cr - Profit
  "   "   "   =   "   if its | Dr Loss